Self-Study Guide
MANAGEMENT

Third Edition

Certified Professional Secretary® Self-Study Guides

Betty L. Schroeder, *Series Editor*

Schroeder, Clark, and DiMarzio Lewis, Webber *Certified Professional Secretary® Review for Business Law,* Third Edition

Cherry *Self-Study Guide to CPS® Review for Finance and Business Law,* Third Edition

Schroeder and Kardoff *Certified Professional Secretary ® Review for Management,* Third Edition

Cherry *Self-Study Guide to CPS® Review for Management,* Third Edition

Schroeder and Routhier Graf *Certified Professional Secretary® Review for OfficeSystems and Administration,* Third Edition

Cherry *Self-Study Guide to CPS® Review for OfficeSystems and Administration,* Third Edition

CERTIFIED PROFESSIONAL SECRETARY®
SELF-STUDY GUIDES

MANAGEMENT
Third Edition

Janet A. Cherry, CPS
The University of Memphis
Memphis, Tennessee

A joint publication of
PSI® Professional Secretaries International and

PRENTICE HALL CAREER & TECHNOLOGY
Englewood Cliffs, New Jersey 07632

The following are trademarks owned by Professional Secretaries International®

TRADEMARKS AND REGISTERED SERVICE MARKS

PSI®
Professional Secretaries International™
Since 1942 known as The National Secretaries Association (International)
10502 N.W. Ambassador Drive, Kansas City, MO 64153 (816) 891-6600

A.I.S.P. (French equivalent of PSI®)
l'Association Internationale des Secretaries Professionailles

CPS®
Certified Professional Secretary®
Professional Secretaries Week®
Professional Secretaries Day®
The Secretary®

FSA®
Future Secretaries Association®
International Secretary of the Year®
Collegiate Secretaries International®

©1995 by PRENTICE HALL Career & Technology
Prentice-Hall, Inc.
A Paramount Communications Company
Englewood Cliffs, New Jersey 07632

Printed in the United States of America

10 9 8 7 6 5 4 3 2

ISBN 0-13-315458-0

Prentice-Hall International (UK) Limited, *London*
Prentice-Hall of Australia Pty. Limited, *Sydney*
Prentice Hall Canada, Inc., *Toronto*
Prentice-Hall Hispanoamericana, S.A., *Mexico City*
Prentice-Hall of India, Private Limited, *New Delhi*
Prentice-Hall of Japan, Inc., *Tokyo*
Simon & Schuster Asia Ptc. Ltd., *Singapore*
Editora Prentice-Hall do Brasil, Ltda., *Rio de Janeiro*

CONTENTS

Suggestions for Using This Self-Study Guide, xi
Additional Suggestions for Preparing for the CPS® Exam, xii
To The CPS® Candidate, xiii
Acknowledgements, xiii
Introduction, xiv

SECTION I: BEHAVIORAL SCIENCE IN BUSINESS

1 Understanding the Individual/Self, 1

Ability and Personality, 1
Values and Attitudes, 4
Emotional Adjustment--Defense/Coping
     Mechanisms, 5
Heredity, Environment, and Stages of Development, 7
Perception and Attribution Theory, 8
Motivation, 9
Theories of Motivation, 10

2 Team Dynamics, 18

Types of Groups, 18
Characteristics of Groups, 21
Advantages and Disadvantages of Groups
     and Teams, 22
Working Effectively with Groups and Teams, 23

3 Leadership Dynamics, 27

Leadership and Leaders, 27
Leadership and Power, 27

Early Approaches to Leadership, 28
Contingency Leadership Approaches, 31
Contemporary Leadership Dimensions, 33
Leadership Effectiveness, 34

4 Interpersonal Communications, 38

Understanding Communication, 38
Forms, Directions, and Types of Communication, 40
Methods of Interpersonal Communication, 43
Barriers to Effective Communication, 45
New Communication Technologies, 48

5 Managing Change, 52

The Nature of Change, 52
Types, Areas, and Directions of Change, 54
The Change Process, 58
Responses to Change, 58
Effective Change Management, 61

SECTION II: HUMAN RESOURCE MANAGEMENT

6 Staffing, 67

The Impact of Women in the Labor Force, 67
Predicting Future Human Resource Needs, 67
Job Analyses, Job Descriptions, Job Specifications,
    and Job Evaluation, 68
Recruitment and Selection, 69

7 Compensation and Benefits, 76

Compensation Administration, 76
Employee Benefits, 78
Major Legislation Affecting Compensation
    and Benefits, 79
Rewards for Employee Involvement, 81

8 Training and Development, 85

Learning--A General Overview, 85
Principles of Learning, 88
Training for Learning, 89
Development Programs for Learning, 92
Evaluating Training Effectiveness, 93

9 Employee Safety, Health, and Stress, 98

Employee Health Concerns and Complaints, 98
Responsibility for Health and Safety, 100
Stress, 101
The Cycle of Stress, 102
Causes of Stress, 102
Stress as an Additive Phenomenon, 103
Manifestations of Stress, 103
Stress Management Techniques, 105

10 Performance Appraisal, 109

The Employee Evaluation Process, 109
Types of Performance Appraisal Systems, 109
Problems in Employee Performance Appraisals, 110

11 Employee-Labor Relations, 114

Major Legislation Affecting Employee-Labor
    Relations, 114
Union-Management Relations, 115
Employee Participation Systems, 116

12 Grievances, Discipline, and Counseling, 120

Discipline, 120
Administration of Discipline, 120
Grievances in Nonunionized Settings, 121
Grievances in Unionized Settings, 121
Grievance Impasse Resolution Methods, 12

13   Employee Separation Processes, 126

Separation, 126
Responsibility for Separation, 126
Legal Separations, 126
Documentation of Separations, 127

SECTION III: ORGANIZATIONS AND MANAGEMENT

14   Principles and Theories of Management, 131

Classical Management Theories, 131
Human Resource Management Theory, 135
Management Science Theory, 138
Total Quality Management, 138

15   Decision-Making Processes, 146

Organizational Decision Making, 146
Logical Reasoning Process, 147

16   The Functions of Management, 152

Planning, 152
Organizing, 154
Leading, 156
Controlling, 158
Communicating, 163

17   Production Management, 173

Facilities, 173
Materials--Procurement, Processing, and Control, 174
Methods and Quality Control, 176
Planning and Scheduling Production, 177

18   Marketing Management, 182

   Marketing Policy, 182
   Implementation of the Marketing Concept/Marketing
      Mix, 182
   Advertising, 186
   Sales Analysis and Control, 187
   Market Analysis, 188
   Traffic Management, 189

   PLANNING SHEET
   S.T.E.P.
   FAST FACT CARDS

SUGGESTIONS FOR USING THIS SELF-STUDY GUIDE

This Self-Study Guide is written as a companion tool rather than as a formally structured workbook. Suggested answers have NOT been included with this material. The purpose of this Self-Study Guide is to assist you in researching and building your own information bank.

The Self-Study Guide is your special workbook to put in writing the information you have acquired through the Prentice Hall CPS® Review Modules and other sources you have selected. Relax and pace yourself according to your individual study plan. Review the material as often as you need. Reinforcement will play a big part in your preparation for the examination.

The material in the Self-Study Guide may be used for independent study and in accelerated, short-term group review courses. Procedures for using the guide in either situation follow.

Independent Study

1.   Introduce yourself to the materials by scanning the Prentice Hall CPS® Review Module and the related materials in this Self-Study Guide.

2.   Read the first section of the related Prentice Hall CPS® Review Module. Then follow the instructions in the Self-Study Guide when you feel comfortable with the text material. The format of the Self-Study Guide allows you to pace yourself through the exercises. By writing your answers, you will be reinforcing your awareness of specific facts in each section. If certain items are confusing to you, return to the CPS® Review Module or other printed resources for additional information or clarification. For additional reinforcement, read the material again. Use the completed Self-Study Guide for review and reinforcement of information. The Self-Study Guide should become your personal reference guide. Recognition and association recall will bring rich dividends on examination day.

3.   **S-T-E-P** through a daily review. Make copies of the **S-T-E-P** (**S**tudy **T**ip **E**xam **P**rep) cards which are found in the back of this Self-Study Guide. Keep the copies with you at all times--in your pockets, beside your bed, in your car, and at your desk. Learn three facts about each term on the cards. Record the terms on a cassette tape leaving time between words for you to mentally give definitions and facts about each, and play the tapes at home or in your car for drill and reinforcement.

4.   **FastFact** cards are also in the back of this Self-Study Guide. Remove the cards and cut them into pocket-size cards along the lines provided. Use the cards to help you become familiar with terminology from the CPS® Review Module. Record the information from the cards onto a cassette tape, and play the tape for reinforcement.

Accelerated Group Review Course

The materials contained in this Self-Study Guide are also a valuable study tool for formal or informal groups. Informal groups might include noon, evening, or intense weekend study sessions.

The informal groups usually function best when the leadership role is shared. A workable plan is to allow each participant to volunteer for a particular section of the CPS® Outline and Bibliography. The section leader provides information to the group about each outline topic--try to provide three facts about each topic. Group members should also rotate as moderators for a quiz on terminology using either the **FastFact** cards or the **S-T-E-P** cards.

It's time to begin. **GOOD LUCK!**

ADDITIONAL SUGGESTIONS FOR PREPARING FOR THE CPS® EXAM...

CONGRATULATIONS! You are on your way. Here are some additional tips that have helped other candidates prepare for the examination:

• Read the advertisements that are directed to you or your executive. In other words, collect junk mail. Ask coworkers to save junk mail for you. This literature contains state-of-the-art terminology, research information, and product news. Take advantage of this convenient resource.

• Prepare a notebook with tabs for each section of the examination. As you see pertinent information or articles that relate, put them into your notebook for review.

• Collect copies of catalogues. Computer and office-supply catalogues are especially good.

• Prepare a weekly quiz. Make it an oral quiz and record the answers on tape for review.

• Take opportunities to attend trade shows, seminars, and workshops on information relative to examination topics.

• Practice to improve your speedreading and comprehension abilities.

• Use the library. A tip on printed materials--check the publication date, particularly in the areas of Office Technology and Office Administration, where changes occur daily. Don't read "dated" materials. The test will reference the latest vocabulary and techniques.

• Certain business-related periodicals and publications are available at no cost if they are ordered on company letterhead. If your office is already receiving such publications, have your name added to the routing list. They will help you to prepare.

• Be prepared to deal with negative reactions you might encounter. Stay in control of your decisions, your time, and your career goals. The CPS® rating is an excellent investment in yourself.

• If you know a secretary who has earned the CPS® rating, enlist this person as your mentor. Arrange a HOT LINE for instant support and encouragement as you pursue your goal.

• Don't procrastinate! Outline a study plan and STICK TO IT! Stay current with your review topics. The week of the examination will come before you know it--YOU WILL BE READY IF YOU WORK AT PREPARING FOR THE EXAM ONE DAY AT A TIME.

Deadlines for filing applications to take the CPS® Examination are September 1 for the November exam and March 1 for the May exam. Applications are available without charge from:

Professional Secretaries International®
P.O. Box 20404
Kansas City, MO 64195-0404

816/891-6600

TO THE CPS® CANDIDATE...

CONGRATULATIONS on your decision to become a Certified Professional Secretary®!

The materials in this Self-Study Guide were prepared to follow the outline and bibliography published by The Institute for Certification, a department of Professional Secretaries International®. This is one of the three Self-Study Guides in the series--there is one for each of the three CPS® Review Modules published by Prentice Hall in conjunction with Professional Secretaries International®.

The information in each of the Self-Study Guides is intended to help you to focus your study of the material in the review modules. Use the information to become more familiar with the terminology, associations, similarities, and differences in the material in the three-part series.

The primary objective of any review course or of any review manual is to serve as a "mental mixer" to bring to the surface certain knowledge, skills, and abilities that may have become subconsciously stored away. It is expected that a candidate for the CPS® Exam would possess the basic fundamentals and skills related to topics covered in each module. If this knowledge base is not present, you may consider enrolling in an introductory course at a post-secondary institution to develop that base.

The Self-Study Guides should be used in conjunction with the appropriate CPS® Review Modules.

ACKNOWLEDGMENTS

It is with pride and pleasure that I am associated with office professionals who have the Certified Professional Secretary rating as one of their career goals. It is because of such dedication to personal achievement that the Self-Study Series was developed. The overall acceptance of the earlier editions of the Self-Study Guides has been positive and encouraging. The synergy created by many caring people contributed to this project. To all who have offered suggestions for improvement, and particularly to the following individuals, I owe tremendous gratitude.

The instructors and candidates who have reviewed and used the materials and provided valuable feedback.

The Institute for Certification, Sister Paulette Gladis, Ph.D., and the International Board of Professional Secretaries International for their interest in and support of these materials;

Elizabeth Sugg and her staff at Prentice Hall for their patience and guidance throughout this project;

Tally Morgan at Wordcrafters for pulling me through this revision;

Thomas Watters, Executive Director, and the PSI® staff;

Ann Brock, CPS, Administrative Assistant, Institute for Executive Education, The University of Memphis, whose enthusiasm for learning has given me new energy;

Lillie T. Lewis, CPS, Administrative Aide, Personnel Services, The University of Tennessee, Memphis, for her dedication and sense of professionalism in keyboarding and formatting this edition;

Secretaries across the United States, Canada, Malaysia, Singapore, the Bahamas, and other parts of the world who have complimented, critiqued, and used the Self-Study Series. You are my inspiration to research, rewrite, and hopefully improve these materials with each edition; and,

The person who introduced me to National Secretaries Association (PSI), served as my role model for a professional secretary, encouraged me to earn my certification and to stay involved and to whom this series is dedicated, my mother.

INTRODUCTION

MANAGEMENT

This part of the examination is particularly interesting inasmuch as it allows you to take a very close look at yourself and your relationships with others. In order to understand our peers, supervisors, and subordinates in the organizational structure it is first necessary to know and understand ourselves.

Each of us is unique and possesses a set of personality traits, attitudes, and emotions that determine our behavior. We use these characteristics to adjust to and survive in our environments and in our dealing with other individuals.

The material in this Self-Study Guide introduces individual behavior patterns, the interdependencies of groups and organizations, the theories of motivation and leadership, the realities of learning, the constancy of change, the bridges and barriers of effective communication, the policies and procedures of effective human resource process; and finally, the theories, principles, and functions of management.

These sections contain valuable information that will assist each of us in living a happy, self-fulfilling life-- both as individuals and business professionals.

Janet T. Cherry, CPS

CHAPTER 1: UNDERSTANDING THE INDIVIDUAL/SELF

In order to be effective in our work relationships and our jobs it is necessary to have a clear understanding of ourselves and others. Human behavior is not always predictable; however, the theories and processes in this section will assist our understanding of self and others. Why we do what we do is interesting to study.

The "self" is defined as the sum of the ideas, beliefs, values, and attitudes that we label "I" or "you." How we think of ourselves affects the way others think of us.

Ability and Personality

The two basic concepts related to self are **ability** and **personality.**

An individual's abilities are comprised primarily of _____and _____abilities.

Those capacities required to perform mental tasks are known as _____abilities. Abilities of this type are more often needed as one rises higher within an organizational hierachy.

Those capacities required to perform tasks requiring energy, dexterity, and strength are known as _____ abilities and are usually among those required at lower levels of an organization.

Ability without effort equals lack of performance and result in failure.

Personality is the sum of the ways that an individual will interact with others and react to others. Primary factors that determine an individual's personality are:

1.   2.   3.

Name three physical traits that have been determined to be a direct result of heredity:

1.   2.   3.

Norms, cultures, and birth order are three environmental forces known to directly affect the ways in which an individual reacts to others. Make a statement about each.

Norms

Culture

Birth order

Personality dimensions include:

1.

2.

3.

4.

5.

6.

Explain the difference in **source** traits and **surface** traits.

When people believe that they have full control over their own destiny and can get whatever they want if they work hard enough, they possess an ( ) internal ( ) external locus of control.

When people believe that all their behaviors are controlled by fate or luck, they possess an ( ) internal ( ) external locus of control.

Risk propensity means . . .

McClelland identified three acquired needs, one of which is dominant in every person at any given time. These needs are:

1.

2.

3.

2

Jung, Myers and **Briggs,** and others found four basic sets of personality dimensions that all persons possess. Make a statement about each.

Introversion/extroversion

Intuition/sensing

Thinking/feeling

Judging/perceiving

The **Myers-Briggs** type indicator identifies _____ distinct personality type classifications.

Holland's Vocational Preference Inventory identified _____ personality types. Holland's types are:

Typical characteristics of a Type A personality are:

Machiavellianism is . . .

Basic approaches used in evaluating personalities include:

1.

2.

3.

The Roschach Inkblot test is an example of _____ tests.

Values and Attitudes

Matching

_____	**1.** attitude	**a.**	expression of our attitude.
_____	**2.** belief	**b.**	cognitive--involving thoughts and knowledge about an object.
_____	**3.** opinion	**c.**	worth placed on an object.
_____	**4.** behavior	**d.**	feelings held about other people and objects.
_____	**5.** value	**e.**	action toward an object.

The worth, merit, or esteem that a person places on various objects helps define that individual's

_____ _____.

The **three** main sources that influence individual value systems are:

1.

2.

3.

Allport and his associates were able to identify a typology of six values. They are:

1.

2.

3.

4.

4

5.

6.

Attitudes reflect individual feelings about other people and things. Attitudes are ( ) more ( ) less stable and enduring than values.

Values and _____ differ among people. Individual differences exist.

A person's general attitude toward his/her job is called _____ _____.

Studies recognize three specific workplace attitudes. The three are:

1.

2.

3.

Emotional Adjustment--Defense/Coping Mechanisms

Emotion is defined as . . .

A person who is emotionally well adjusted recognizes that:

1 .

2.

3.

An emotionally well adjusted person has developed the skills and knowledge necessary for effective judgment and decisions.

Emotions may move a person to action. Emotions can result from events in our environment. Even though emotions can be initiated by the appearance or action of an individual, these feelings are externally initiated. Behaviors are directed by emotions.

Emotions are described as positive or negative, pleasant or unpleasant.

Our emotions can provide the internal **drive** to move us toward an action taking us closer to a goal. When we experience a block (internal or external) in reaching this goal we experience frustration. Tools to assist us in handling frustration are called **defense** or **coping mechanisms**. There are active and passive coping skills.

From the list of common reactions to frustration below, select the active and passive responses and explain each.

Withdrawal	Regression
Rationalization	Substitute Work
Isolation	Fixation
Rumor-Mongering	Aggression
Projection	Resignation
Conscious Hypocrisy	

Active   **Passive**

6

Explain three types of coping behaviors:

Trial and Error

Reshaping the Problem

Revising the Goal

Heredity, Environment, and Stages of Development

Physiologically, emotions trigger the sympathetic nervous system to ready the person for extraordinary action. Every society has patterns of acceptable and unacceptable behavior based on cultural patterns. And, every society has local subunits of acceptable behavior. People adjust in different ways to these conditions while striving to satisfy human needs.

There are two major response patterns:

1.

or

2.

Adults as well as children have clearly defined stages of biological, social, and family development.

Three researchers known for their studies of the stages of individual behavior development are:

1.

2.

3.

7

Their studies revealed:

1.   Personality development based on _____
      _____;

2.   Personality development and the _____process; and,

3.   Personality development stages as _____activities.

Perception and Attribution Theory

Perception is the process by which people . . .

Perception is influenced by situational characteristics. Major situational characteristics include:

1.

2.

3.

4.

5.

6.

7.

Individual perceptions about the behaviors of others are greatly influenced by assumptions made about the reasons for these behaviors, and based on internal or external causes. The Attribution Theory is defined as the process of determining whether behaviors observed in other individuals are _____ or _____ caused.

Explain the term "self-serving bias."

Motivation

Our motives are personal and internal. We can be offered external incentives in hopes of provoking certain actions. If the action matches our felt needs, a person is considered to be motivated.

Motivation can be defined as those factors which cause, channel, and sustain individuals to perform goal-directed actions.

Complete the schematic representation of the motivation process.

NEEDS	MOTIVES	MOTIVATED	
			INTRINSIC GOALS
			EXTRINSIC GOALS

Motivation begins with a need. The two kinds of needs are:

1.

2.

Define the elements involved with the motivational process.

1 .

2.

3.

4.

9

The need-oriented approach to the study of motivation is called _____
_____.

Two types of goals are:

1.

2.

Label the expanded motivational process with emphasis on goals:

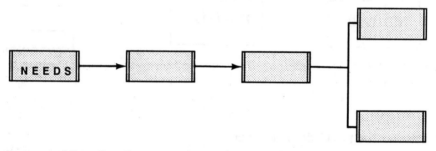

The assignment of the attractiveness value to the reward, or goal, rests in a person's belief (expectations).
The positive degree of attractiveness is referred to as _____.

Theories of Motivation

Contemporary theories of motivation include three basic schools:

Type	Theorist	Theory
Content theory (focuses on the question "what causes people to act in certain ways?")	1. 2. 3. 4.	1. 2. 3. 4.
Process theory (focuses on how people choose their course of action from among alternatives)	1. 2. 3.	1. 2. 3.

10

Type	**Theorist**	**Theory**
Reinforcement Theory (examines how the consequences of past behavior affect future actions)	1. 2.	1. 2.

Explain each of the early motivation models:

Traditional

Human relations

Human resources

Douglas McGregor developed two sets of assumptions regarding how people acted: Theory X and Theory Y. State characteristics of each.

Theory X

Theory Y

Maslow's Hierachy of Needs is based on the premise that psychological growth-fulfilling potential is the dominant motivating force in people. Label and explain the need levels as identified by Abraham Maslow.

Clayton Alderfer's ERG theory, although similar to Maslow's, differs in what three basic ways?

1.

2.

3.

Frederick Herzberg's two-factor theory is based on:

1.

2.

How do these two factors relate to satisfiers and dissatisfiers?

The six primary motivators from Herzberg's theory can be remembered by using the acronym RAW RAG. Complete the acronym:

R_____   R_____
A_____   A_____
W_____   G_____

Frederick Herzberg noted that when deficiences existed in any of the hygiene factors, worker dissatisfaction ( ) would ( ) would not result.

Herzberg also noted that the absence of some motivators ( ) would ( ) would not lead to lack of satisfaction, not dissatisfaction.

David McClelland's Higher Level Needs Theory supports Maslow and Herzberg. His work and theory centered around which level of Maslow's needs scale?

McClelland found that there are three basic types of needs that everyone can acquire during their lifetime. Name and define each type of need.

1.

2.

3.

Explain **Victor Vroom's expectancy theory** of motivation.

Reinforcement theories of motivation can be represented by the following formula:

S_____   R_____   C_____   F_____   R_____

Explained as. . .

Name and explain the **four** types of reinforcement techniques:

1.

2.

3.

4.

Blanchard and Johnson call _____the "breakfast of champions."

The self-fulfilling prophecy (Pygmalion effect) holds that people respond . . .

The self-fulfilling prophecy is based on the following:

1.

2.

3.

4.

State ways that motivational theories may be applied to the work environment.

Supervisory functions

Organizational policies and structures

14

Below is a comparison diagram of the Motivation Theories developed by Maslow, Herzberg, and McClelland. See if you can label them.

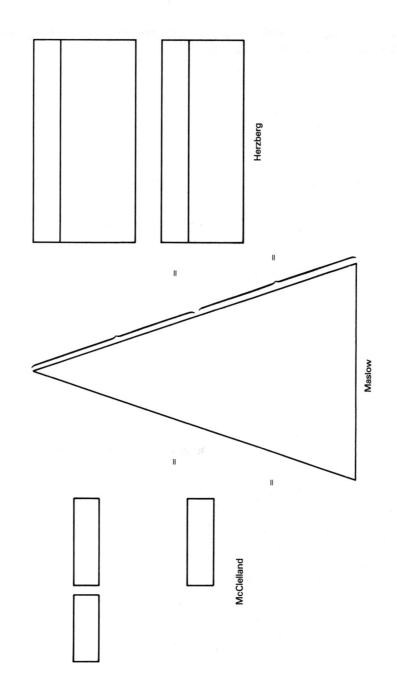

Section I: Behavioral Science in Business
Part III: Management, 1 Hour, 45 Minutes
150 Items, 36% of Part III

15

CHAPTER 1: UNDERSTANDING THE INDIVIDUAL/SELF

Terms and Definitions

Use this page to record terms and definitions you want to concentrate on, or to record additional information you have located from other resources.

CHAPTER 1:   UNDERSTANDING THE INDIVIDUAL/SELF

Additional Comments

Use this page to record information found in readings, notes from lectures, or notes to yourself about topics to be researched.

CHAPTER 2: TEAM DYNAMICS

While each employee is responsible for specific job tasks, it is highly probable that most of these tasks will require interdependency. The interaction with co-workers--one or a group--can be a source of satisfaction or frustration.

All work groups are unique. This is logical because groups are formed by a number of unique individuals coming together for a common goal.

Types of Groups

A group may be defined as:

The **four** components of a **formal** group are:

1.

2.

3.

4.

Name and describe five types of formal groups.

1.

2.

3.

4.

5.

Teams may be classified by _____ or by _____.

A **vertical** team is known as a . . .

Vertical teams are often formed with members of the same _____ _____.

A **horizontal** team is a group of employees . . .

Work teams are often viewed as an extension of _____ _____.

Four facts about special-purpose teams are:

1.

2.

3.

4.

Describe a **self-managing** team.

An **ad hoc** committee is disbanded when . . .

An **informal group** is created by the employees themselves. The components of an informal group are:

1.

2.

3.

4 .

There are two primary types of informal groups:

1.

2.

Memberships in informal groups changes over time to shifts in interests, affiliations, or friendship.

Make a statement about each of the following reasons for forming an informal group.

Affiliation

Mutual aid

Protection

Communication

Proximity

Attraction

Sharing norms and values

Characteristics of Groups

Explain and compare the group characteristics of a formal and an informal group:

Formal	Informal
1.	
2.	
4.	
5.	
6.	

Reasons for status differences in groups include:

1.

2.

3.

4.

Advantages and Disadvantages of Groups and Teams

Advantages

1.

2.

3.

4.

5.

6.

7.

8.

Disavantages

1.

2.

3.

4.

5.

6.

7.

<u>Working Effectively with Groups and Teams</u>

The effectiveness of formal groups and teams can be improved by:

1.

2.

3.

4.

How should the boundaries of group activities be communicated?

Strategies for working cooperatively with informal groups include:

1.

2.

3.

4.

CHAPTER 2: TEAM DYNAMICS

Terms and Definitions

Use this page to record terms and definitions you want to concentrate on, or to record additional information you have located from other resources.

CHAPTER 2:   TEAM DYNAMICS

Additional Comments

Use this page to record information found in readings, notes from lectures, or notes to yourself about topics to be researched.

CHAPTER 2: TEAM DYNAMICS

Additional Comments

CHAPTER 3:   LEADERSHIP DYNAMICS

A **leader** exercises influence over another person's behavior.   A **follower** accepts the leader's instructions and directions because he/she feels the leader is acting appropriately.   Leadership involves guiding, directing, and influencing individual and group behaviors toward achieving specific goals.

Leadership and Leaders

Management refers to the process of . . .

Leaders are concerned with . . .

All managers have to perform the _____function; however, all leaders do not have to perform the _____, _____, or _____ function.

Leadership differs from authority, which is the formal right to command, set group goals, and direct people's efforts to achieve group goals.   Authority relies largely on two concepts:

1.

2.

Responsibilities of leaders ( ) do ( ) do not differ in formal and informal groups.

Leadership and Power

Power is the motivational factor, or force, which provides the leader with the ability to influence others to change their behaviors as the leader desires.

All people do not aspire to be leaders.   Those who have the internal motivation to take the responsibility of leadership channel their capabilities differently.

Name and make a statement about the five types of power at a leader's disposal:

1.

2.

3.

4.

5.

These five types of power may be placed into two general categories--positive and personal power. Make statements about the differences in the two types.

Positive power

Personal power

Looking at power in the terms of Herzbergs's two-factor system, position power can be regarded as a ( ) hygiene ( ) motivational factor and personal power can be regarded as a ( ) hygiene ( ) motivational factor.

Early Approaches to Leadership

Studies can't evidence conclusive facts to show that leaders have similar personality traits. However, studies have shown that the facts below tend to be true regarding task-related characteristics:

1.

2.

3.

4.

5.

6.

In Chapter 2 you were introduced to Douglas McGregor's Theory X and Theory Y. As a review, list the attitude assumptions of each leadership theory:

THEORY X	THEORY Y
1.	1.
2.	2.
3.	3.
4.	4.
	5.

It is important to note that while there are no "right" or "wrong" styles of leadership, there are definite approaches adopted by persons in successful leadership roles. Research has found that with many variations two major behavorial approaches are frequently observed. These are referred to as:

1.   **People-oriented (consideration)**

2 .   **Job-oriented (production-oriented)**

The studies conducted at the University of Michigan and at Ohio State University produced similar evidence. The conclusions were:

1.

2.

3.

4.

5.

The Tannenbaum and Schmidt leadership continuum reflects leadership styles with varying amounts of employee participation and with seven separate leadership approaches ranging from boss-centered to subordinate-centered styles.

The Blake and Mouton Managerial Grid identified five separate leadership styles and proposed that there was one best way to lead people.

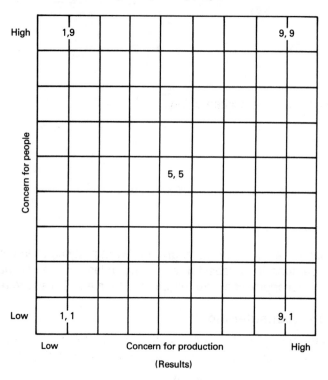

Label the following positions on the grid and indicate the significance of each. Describe the labels listed below from the Managerial Grid:

1,9

9,9

5,5

1,1

9,1

Blake and Mouton observed that the most effective leadership style was _____
_____, 9,9.

30

Contingency Leadership Approaches

The **Law of the Situation** (Follett 1920-30) suggested that leadership effectiveness is primarily the result of an active interaction and interrelationship of three sets of factors. Name these factors.

1.

2.

3.

Briefly describe the contingency models listed below:

Fiedler's Model

Robert House's Path-Goal Theory

Victor Vroom and Phillip Yetton's Leader-Participation Theory. (Vroom and Yetton identified five decision-making styles, each with a certain degree of subordinate participation).

Paul Hersey and Kenneth Blanchard's Life-Cycle (Situational) Theory

The seven basic questions used in the decision tree process are:

1 .

2.

3.

4.

5.

6.

7.

Maturity consists of two separate components. Explain each.

Job-related components

Psychological components

The four levels of maturity most people go through are:

1.

2.

3.

4.

Hersey and Blanchard identified four basic styles of leadership that can be used with the maturity levels.
Make a statement about each of these styles.

Telling

Selling

Participating

Delegating

<u>Contemporary Leadership Dimensions</u>

The psychoanalytic view of leadership states . . .

The romantic view of leadership states . . .

Attribution theory applied to leadership suggests . . .

Inspirational leadership focuses . . .

Inspirational leaders are often called charismatic because of their unique abilities to arouse emotional responses in subordinates. A specific type of inspirational leader is the _____ leader.

Transactional leaders specialize in performing the four traditional management functions and are viewed more like managers.

Specific characteristics of the organization, subordinates, and tasks sometimes serve as general substitutes for leadership. These include:

Organization

Subordinates

Tasks

Self-managed work teams and self-leadership often result in:

1.

2.

3.

4.

Why has the self-managed work team concept come into existence?   What are the benefits?

Leadership Effectiveness

What has research found as to the possible relationships of leadership style to:

Satisfaction

Productivity

Levels in the organizational hierachy

CHAPTER 3: LEADERSHIP DYNAMICS

Terms and Definitions

Use this page to record terms and definitions you want to concentrate on, or to record additional information you have located from other resources.

CHAPTER 3: LEADERSHIP DYNAMICS

Additional Comments

Use this page to record information found in readings, notes from lectures, or notes to yourself about topics to be researched.

CHAPTER 3: LEADERSHIP DYNAMICS

Additional Comments

CHAPTER 4:   INTERPERSONAL COMMUNICATION

We are always communicating. The signals we use to communicate verbally and nonverbally have tremendous impact on the effectiveness of the communication purpose. Communication is the process of sharing information and meaning, knowingly and unknowingly.

Understanding Communication

Communications are shared messages, symbols, and other types of information sent through a transmission medium.

Reasons for treating communication as an important part of all business functions are:

1.

2.

3.

4.

5.

Communication serves many purposes within an organization. Among the most important are:

1.

2.

3.

4.

5.

6.

7.

Label the communication process model diagramed below:

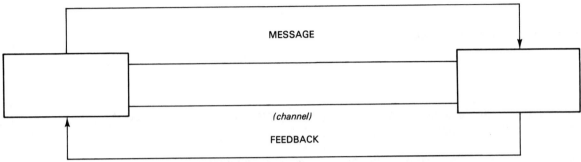

Encoding means . . .

Decoding means . . .

Communication channels include:

1.

2.

3.

4.

5.

Feedback is the receiver s response to the message. Effective feedback is vital but not essential to the communication process for information sharing to be complete.

The communication process is completed when the _____ receives and _____ the message.

Channel noise is a major communication disturbance. Examples of channel noise are:

1.

2.

3.

Explain how "time" is a form of noise.

In the communication process, face-to-face communication provides the most immediate _____;
written communication provides the most _____.

The capacity of a comunication channel is largely determined by what three criteria?

1.

2.

3.

The selection of the appropriate channel is somewhat determined by the amount of time allocated and
the number of receivers.

For a shorter time and a small number of receivers, channel preference is . . .

For intermediate amounts of time and numbers of receivers to be reached, channel preference is . . .

For longer time allowance and larger numbers of receivers to be reached, channel preference is . . .

Explain the meaing of the terms:

Efficient communication

Effective communication

Forms, Directions, and Types of Communication

The term **"serial transmissions"** means . . .

40

The term **"gangplank principle"** means . . .

Name, describe, and give examples of the four formal communication channels which exist within any organization:

1.

2.

3.

4.

The most common type of communication flow is _____.

Possible problems in downward communication are:

1.

2.

3.

4.

5.

Possible problems in upward communication are:

1.

2.

3.

4.

41

Two of the main reasons for lateral communication within an organization are:

1.

2.

Formal communication networks include the following. Make statements about each.

Chain or single stand

Star (where)

Circle

"Y"

All-channel

Each type has advantages and disadvantages and there is no "best" pattern for all circumstances. The contingency approach is the best method to use in selecting a network pattern.

When time is crucial, the _____ pattern is best.

The _____ is the slowest network .

The _____, _____, and _____ are all effective when accuracy is essential.

The _____ allows for the greatest amount of information distortion.

There is no formal leadership in the _____ or _____ networks.

When subordinate satisfaction is desired, the _____ and _____ networks are best. The _____ is least effective.

The _____ is the most common informal communication channel. The main purpose of this channel is to . . .

"MBWA" is both an informal and formal communication channel, as well as being a formalized management technique. What does 'MBWA' stand for? Explain the concept.

The four basic personal communication styles are:

1.

2.

3.

4.

The most effective form is _____.

Methods of Interpersonal Communication

The primary methods of interpersonal communication involve:

1.

2.

3.

The most common form of organizational communication is _____.

Nonverbal communication is the process of sharing information without the use of words. Messages are transmitted through body movements, office layout, appearance, tone of voice, and facial expression.

The ( ) verbal ( ) nonverbal message has greater credibility.

The most prominent forms of nonverbal communication are:

1.

2.

3.

4.

5.

Name and define the four distance zones in nonverbal communication.

1.

2.

3.

4.

Give examples of "object" language.

1.

2.

3.

4.

5.

6.

Barriers to Effective Communication

Define two types of mechanisms that can be used to assess organizational communication effectiveness:

The communication audit

The communication effectiveness index

Communication barriers can be divided into organization barriers, interpersonal barriers, and personal barriers.

The more common organizational barriers include:

1.

2.

3.

4.

5.

6.

7.

Make a statement about each of the following types of interpersonal communication barrier.

Stereotyping

Status

Noise

45

Poor listening

Difference in language and culture

Semantics

Improper channel selection

Personal differences among individuals also may result in communication barriers. These differences may result from education, experience, or attitude.

The greatest cause of communication problems is the result of differences in _____.

Techniques for improving communication in organizations include:

1.

2.

3.

4 .

Methods for improving interpersonal communication include:

1.

2.

3.

4.

5.

6.

7.

8.

9.

Methods for improving personal communication include:

1.

2.

3.

4.

5.

6.

7.

8.

9 .

Active listening is the process of . . .

Active listening is a skill and depends upon the mindset and willingness of the listener to perceive, participate, and personalize the message "internally."

Some of the more common ways of improving listening effectiveness in business settings include:

1.

2.

47

3.

4.

5.

6.

7.

8.

9.

10.

New Communication Technologies

Advances in technology have had dramatic effects on certain types of communication. Advances have made communication easier, more timely, and more accurate while eliminating distance barriers and improving the speed, and the associated services.

Some of the more recent innovations now influencing communication in the workplace are:

1.

2.

3.

4.

5.

6 .

7.

CHAPTER 4:   INTERPERSONAL COMMUNICATION

Terms and Definitions

Use this page to record terms and definitions you want to concentrate on, or to record additional information you have located from other resources.

CHAPTER 4:   INTERPERSONAL COMMUNICATION

Additional Comments

Use this page to record information found in readings, notes from lectures, or notes to yourself about topics to be researched.

CHAPTER 4: INTERPERSONAL COMMUNICATION

Additional Comments

CHAPTER 5:   MANAGING CHANGE

Our existence is based on change.   As individuals, each day of life gives us a new perspective and sets of experiences with which to make decisions, solve problems, and create new sets of circumstances. A major task is to **PLAN** for and **MANAGE** this change. If we can direct our energy toward change management, we can eliminate potential stress and enjoy a more productive life. Change is exciting to some people and threatening to others. In fact, change may be **both** exciting and threatening.

The Nature of Change

Change is the process of making things different. Organizational change is . . .

Change is necessary because . . .

Change in individuals is due to:

1.

2.

Typical organizational life cycle stages are:

1.

2.

3.

4.

5.

Change is both individual and organizational. Personal change affects the organization and organizational change affects the individual.

Use the space below to indicate the forces of external and internal change within the organization.

External	**Internal**
1.	1.
2.	2.
3.	3.
4.	4.
5.	5.
	6.
	7.
	8.
	9.
	1 0.

External forces are more important because they are ( ) more ( ) less subject to organizational and managerial control.

The three types of organizational response to change are given below. Explain each:

Planned change

Reactive change

Doing nothing to change

53

Another term for planned change is _____change.

Which of the three types of change responses is preferred? Why?

Types, Areas, and Direction of Change

Change is needed when a review of external or internal factors that cause change reveals that a difference exists between desired and actual levels of performance.

The difference between actual and desired levels of performance is called a _____ _____.

This difference can occur for one or more of the following reasons:

1.

2.

3.

4.

When deficiencies exist in the worker's performance skills or attitudes or in the effectiveness of the managers, this may be the result of:

1.

2.

3.

4.

5.

6.

Most errors are made in determining the need for change by. . .

When evaluating the need for change, the consideration of responses to four basic questions will generally provide the needed information. What are these four basic questions?

The traditional decision-making mode, applied to change-solving, as stated in your text lists seven steps. These steps are:

Step 1:

Step 2:

Step 3:

Step 4:

Step 5:

Step 6:

Step 7:

The **two** basic types of change are **incremental** and **strategic.** Explain the difference between the two types.

Incremental change

Strategic change

Four basic categories within which planned changes can occur are **structural, technological, new product** and **behavioral.** Make statements about each category.

Structural change

Technological change

New product change

Behavioral change

The primary focus of people change is on such factors as:

1.

2.

3.

Organizational development (OD) is defined as . . .

People changes can be introduced by top-level, middle-level, first-line managers, or even the workers themselves.

A **change agent** is . . .

The **role** of a change agent is . . .

Name and define the four most common types of change agents.

1.

2.

3.

4.

Four basic approaches used by management to implement proposed changes include the top-down (unilateral); limited involvement of subordinates; joint-manager-worker; and the bottoms-up approach. Give advantages and disadvantages of each as given in your text.

Approach Type	Advantages	Disadvantages
Top-down		
Limited manager-worker involvement		
Joint participation		
Bottoms-up		

The Change Process

The three-step change model developed by Kurt Lewin in 1951 is widely accepted in the business world. The three steps are identified below. Explain each of these steps:

Unfreezing

Changing (or moving)

Refreezing

Lewin also found from his studies that every behavior was the result of an interaction of two sets of opposite factors. Name and explain these factors.

1.

2.

Force-field analysis is the process of determining those forces that support movements for change and those forces that oppose any changes.

Responses to Change

Responses to change vary; however, the **three types** of responses to change are:

1.

2.

3.

People resist change for many different reasons. Explain the reasons for resistance listed below:

Uncertainty

Threatened self-interests

Feelings of personal loss

Conflicting perceptions of proposed changes

Economic reasons

Fear of failure

Change of habit

Social factors

Lack of trust

Loss of face

Need for status quo

Organizations also resist change for many different reasons. Some specific reasons are listed below. Explain these reasons:

Overdetermination or structural inertia

Group inertia

Threatened expertise

Threatened shifts in power

Narrow change of focus

Potential loss of resources

Previously unsuccessful change efforts

Managers and acquisitions

Downsizing

Participative management

Poor timing of changes

Surprise

Name the most recognized methods people express for resisting change.

1.

2.

3.

4.

Management by Walking Around means . . .

Effective Change Management

Change should be closely monitored. Factors of significant importance are:

1.

2.

3.

It is recognized that supporters of the change process are important players. What can managers do to encourage change supporters to remain enthusiastic?

Those who are undecided about changes also need attention. What can be done to attempt to prevent these people from joining the opponents to given proposed changes?

61

General practices which may be utilized to reduce the resistance to change include:

1.

2.

3.

4.

5.

6.

Definitive strategies for dealing with resistance to change are listed below. Make statements about each.

Education and communication

Participation and involvement

Facilitation and support

Negotiation and agreement

Manipulation and cooptation

Explicit and implicit coercion

Organizational development (OD) was introduced earlier in this chapter.   It is a popular approach for working with organizational change. The basic requirements for effective OD programs include:

1.

2.

3.

4.

5 .

The primary objectives of OD are:

1.

2.

3.

4.

5.

6.

7.

OD intervention strategies aimed at changing the attitudes and behavior of organizational members basically involve communication, decision making, and problem solving processes. Other options are often used and your text listed several of these. List these options below:

While OD research is yet inconclusive as to the evidence of its effectiveness, it is a helpful tool to use when an organization needs to review its strength and weaknesses, opportunities and threats (SWOT). OD also offers assistance to managers in

- introducing planned organizational changes;

- fostering creativity and innovation;

- improving organizational productivity; and

- enhancing individual and overall organizational effectiveness.

CHAPTER 5: MANAGING CHANGE

Terms and Definitions

Use this page to record terms and definitions you want to concentrate on, or to record additional information you have located from other resources.

CHAPTER 5: MANAGING CHANGE

Additional Comments

Use this page to record information found in readings, notes from lectures, or notes to yourself about topics to be researched.

CHAPTER 5: MANAGING CHANGE

Additional Comments

CHAPTER 6: STAFFING

People are an organization's most valuable asset. Ongoing efforts must be taken to make wise selections, and care for those selected from the day of employment to the day of retirement or resignation.

The Impact of Women in the Labor Force

Women represent about one-half of the total work force; however, their salaries are still only about _____ percent of those received by men. Almost _____ percent of all mothers are employed now.

In the year 2000, the U.S. labor force will be about 140 million people. The number of Americans between the ages of 35 and 54 will dramatically ( ) increase ( ) decrease when other age groups will grow in business far more slowly or decline in numbers. Women now make up over _____ percent of all individuals in the professions.

In the United States more than _____ percent of working women are in the information industries.

Education continues as a key factor of employment, _____, and retention.

The Small Business Administration estimates that by the year 2000 about _____percent of all small businesses will be headed by women.

The two-paycheck families have become the norm in our society. This factor increases the needs of working families for child care and elder care. Among programs which support this need are:

1.

2.

3.

4.

Predicting Future Human Resource Needs

The process of identifying future human resource needs involves:

1.

2.

3.

4.

Human resource forecasting involves studying:

1.

2.

The Delphi technique is one methhod used in predicting human resource needs. List the steps and explain the process used in applying the Delphi Technique.

Job Analyses, Job Descriptions, Job Specifications, and Job Evaluation

A **job analysis is . . .**

The job analysis formula is . . .

The **job description** ( ) should ( ) should not be in writing.

The job description should be as specific as possible.

The **job specification** serves as a blueprint for . . .

Of the three--job analysis, job description, or job specification--which is usually most susceptible to review in terms of equal employment opportunity or affirmative action?

The job _____ serves as the basis for determining the skills necessary in the people who will be hired to fill the positions.

Task analysis is . . .

Time and motion-study is generally discussed as a part of scientific management. The four significant concerns of time and motion study are:

1.

2.

3.

4.

"MTM" means . . .

Some ways that task analyses may be conducted are:

1.

2.

3.

Recruitment and Selection

Recruitment is the process of . . .

Advantages of recruiting from within include:

1.

2.

3.

4.

5.

Disadvantages of recruiting from within include:

1.

2.

3.

4.

5.

A **job evaluation** is a carefully designed program for:

1.

2.

Three factors often included in job evaluations are:

1.

2.

3.

Sources for external recruiting include:

1.

2.

3.

4.

5.

6.

7.

8.

Six common methods or criteria for employee selection are:

1.

2.

3.

4.

5.

6.

Legislation prohibiting employers with _____ or more employees from implementing personnel practices which discriminate on the basis of race, color, sex, national origin, or religion are named below. List the primary provisions of each of the legislative acts named below:

Age Discrimination in Employment Act (1967)

Equal Employment Opportunity Act (1972)

Vocational Rehabilitation Act (1973)

The Equal Pay Act (1963)

The Americans with Disabilities Act (1990)

CHAPTER 6: STAFFING

Terms and Definitions

Use this page to record terms and definitions you want to concentrate on, or to record additional information you have located from other resources.

CHAPTER 6: STAFFING

Additional Comments

Use this page to record information found in readings, notes from lectures, or notes to yourself about topics to be researched.

CHAPTER 6: STAFFING

Additional Comments

CHAPTER 7:   COMPENSATION AND BENEFITS

Wage and salary administration present one of the most complex and difficult functions of personnel management. The costs of health care, the increasing numbers of part-time employees, and other benefit programs have contributed to the complexity of the compensation and benefits areas.

<u>Compensation Administration</u>

Components of large wage and salary departments may include:

1.

2.

3.

4.

5.

6.

7.

If ideal, a compensation plan would be designed to meet the requirements of both employer and employee. These objectives are:

1.

2.

3.

4.

5.

6.

7.

The **two** basic types of compensation plans are **direct** and **indirect**. Define these two plans:

Direct

Indirect

What is the difference between a **straight** salary and an **output-based** salary?

Straight salary

Output-based salary

Indirect compensation is a form of tax-free income. As much as _____ percent of the employee's total salary may be in the form of indirect compensation or fringe benefits.

Indirect compensation required by law includes:

1.

2.

3.

4 .

The **primary** types of optional indirect compensation are in the following five major areas:

1.

2.

3.

4.

5.

Special compensation items provided for many company executives often include:

1.

2.

3.

4.

5.

6.

7.

Exempt "personnel" include . . .

Compensation for nonexempt personnel may be referred to as _____. Hourly workers are customarily paid each _____.

Compensation for exempt personnel may be referred to as _____.

The **Fair Labor Standards Act**, also known as the _____ _____ _____ _____, governs . . .

The **Equal Pay Act** (1963) states that . . .

Employee Benefits

Make statements about the administration and provisions of the following state and federal laws:

Federal Social Security Act

Workers' compensation laws

Unemployment insurance (UI)

Benefit programs do contribute to recruiting and retaining competent employees. Optional types of indirect compensation include:

1.

2.

3.

4.

5.

6.

7.

8.

9.

10.

11.

Explain the term **"cafeteria style of indirect compensation."**

The "salary reduction plan" is known commonly as a _____plan. This plan allows a company to . . .

Major Legislation Affecting Compensation and Benefits

Equal opportunity refers to . . .

The Equal Pay Act (1963) prohibits . . .

Title VII of the Civil Rights Act (1964) was amended by the EEO Act of 1972. EEO provisions pertain to virtually all _____ and _____.

The doctrine of comparable worth states that . . .

This doctrine ( ) has ( ) has not been accepted as official law by the U.S. Government.

The Pregnancy Discrimination Act (1978) prohibits . . .

Age Discrimination in Employment Act (1967) . . .

Mandatory Retirement Act (1974) . . .

Employee Retirement Income Society Act (ERISA) (1974) . . .

Veterans Readjustment Act (1974) . . .

Vocational Rehabilitation Act (1973). . .

Social Security Act (1935) as amended . . .

Fair Labor Standards Act (1938) as amended . . .

Health Maintenance Organization Act (HMO) (1973) . . .

If state and local laws are in place and more rigid than the federal law, they have to be followed. Three areas to be mentioned are:

1.

2.

3.

Rewards for Employee Involvement

Monetary rewards for employees who offer suggestions include:

1.

2.

3.

4.

Nonmonetary incentives might include:

1.

2.

3.

4.

5.

CHAPTER 7: COMPENSATION AND BENEFITS

Terms and Definitions

Use this page to record terms and definitions you want to concentrate on, or to record additional information you have located from other resources.

CHAPTER 7: COMPENSATION AND BENEFITS

Additional Comments

Use this page to record information found in readings, notes from lectures, or notes to yourself about topics to be researched.

CHAPTER 7:   COMPENSATION AND BENEFITS

Additional Comments

CHAPTER 8: TRAINING AND DEVELOPMENT

Learning is a lifelong process caused by a change in behavior resulting from practice and experience. The importance of continuous learning for the manager or for the professional secretary cannot be overstated.

Learning--A General Overview

- Learning involves long-lasting changes;

- Learning involves changes in the way a person behaves;

- Learning, as with any change, may lead to resistance;

- Learning is a process; and

- Learning and maturation are distinctly different.

Learning can occur in any of three general domains (Bloom's taxonomy) These demains are:

- Cognitive
- Affective
- Psychomotor

In the cognitive domain there are five learning outcomes. Name these five outcomes in their proper hierachy and make a statement about each.

1.

2.

3.

4.

5.

Learning is indicated by . . .

1.

2.

3.

. . . and also includes interpersonal communication and the shaping of feelings and emotions with others.

This type of learning expressed by the actual performance of particular acts is realized through the
_____domain.

The most common formal learning theories include:

1.

2.

3.

4.

Classical conditioning is a(n) ( ) active ( ) passive way of learning. This theory refers to learning that has occurred when a living organism responds to a stimulus that ( ) would ( ) would not normally produce such a response.

Who discovered classical conditioning?

What did his experiments involve?

In essence, this theory involves building up an association between a conditioned _____
and an unconditioned _____.

Operant conditioning is also known as the Law of _____. The premise of this theory is that behavior results from its _____.

Operant behavior is a ( ) voluntary ( ) involuntary behavior. Behaviors that are rewarded tend to be
_____, while behaviors that are ignored or punished tend to be
_____.

Who is the founder of operant conditioning?

Cognitive learning focuses on _____ things are done, not _____ things are done.

Cognitive learning also examines how people pursue desired goals, interpret work tasks as opportunities to satisfy desires, and reduce perceived inequities.

Social learning is also known as _____ learning. Social learning involves role and behavioral modeling by observing and following the action of others.

Social learning may be viewed as an extension of _____conditioning in that it functions through the law of effect.

People are most influenced by models who are:

1.

2.

3.

What does a **learning curve** indicate?

The slope of the learning curve represents . . .

   a graduated slope . . .

   a steep slope . . .

   a typical slope . . .

A **learning plateau** represents . . .

The **asymptote** is the . . .

Two basic approaches to learning are:

1.

2.

_____is the instructional approach used by children; _____ is the instructional approach used with adults and nontraditional learners.

All persons tend to use one of the four basic learning styles.   List characteristics of each of these four styles:

1.

2.

3.

4.

Principles of Learning

In order for learning to be effective in the training and development arena, two preconditions must exist:

1.

2.

The motivational learning levels of traditional students are often ( ) low ( ) high. The motivational learning levels of adults or nontraditional students are often ( ) low ( ) high.

Self-efficacy expectations are:

The theory of early successes is a form of _____ conditioning.

Make statements about each of the learning principles listed below:

Feedback

Reinforcement

Practice

Overcoming interference

Transfer of learning

Relevance of material

Conditions for learning

Training for Learning

Training is the process of providing the opportunity for individuals to gain knowledge, skills, and attitudes required in their **present** jobs.

Two primary benefits of training are:

1.

2.

The **first step** in designing a training program involves a needs assessment of training needs. The first step in a needs assessment is a _____ _____.

The **second step** involves the study of present and projected job needs. How is this done?

The **third step** involves conducting an employee needs analysis. This includes:

1.

2.

Why do self-assessments of training needs often produce less than factual information?

Task-person analyses are used to evaluate the _____, _____, and _____ required to perform specific tasks and jobs.

Most training programs are oriented toward modifying or improving workers skills in one of three primary categories. Name these categories and make a statement about each.

1.

2.

3.

Basic literacy skill training relates to instruction to correct workers deficiencies in:

1.

2.

3 .

4.

5.

OJT means . . .

Types of OJT include:

1.

2.

3.

4.

5.

Name the variety of training experiences included in on-site/off-job training programs:

1.

2.

3.

4.

5.

Off-the-job site (**OFS**) training programs may include:

1.

2.

3.

4.

5.

6.

7.

8.

Development Programs for Learning

Training focuses on improving skills needed to perform one's present job. **Development** focuses on improving an employee's competence for possible job opportunities in the future.

For the most part, the process of creating a development program follows the training process. The final step in the process is the evaluation phase. Outline below what is evaluated during this step.

The competencies required for first-line, middle, and top-level management are diverse. Basically, the skill emphasis for each level is:

First-line

Middle

Top-level

The Peter Principle applies when . . .

92

Management development programs are designed to improve the effectiveness of the manager's job performance, especially in terms of competence in:

1.

2.

3.

4.

5.

6.

Explain the **"incident process"** as it is applied to management development.

Evaluating Training Effectiveness

A widely accepted method for evaluating training was developed by Donald Kirkpatrick and utilizes four hierachical levels of evaluations. Name and make a statement about each:

1.

2.

3.

4.

93

The most effective training evaluation designs use multiple measures, such as pretests and posttests, and allow for changes in trainees. Name other designs:

1.

2.

3.

CHAPTER 8: TRAINING AND DEVELOPMENT

Additional Comments

Use this page to record terms and definitions you want to concentrate on, or to record additional information you have located from other resources.

CHAPTER 8: TRAINING AND DEVELOPMENT

Additional Comments

Use this page to record information found in readings, notes from lectures, or notes to yourself about topics to be researched.

CHAPTER 8:   TRAINING AND DEVELOPMENT

Additional Comments

CHAPTER 9: EMPLOYEE SAFETY, HEALTH, AND STRESS

Employees expect to work in a safe environment without any major health risk, and without excessive stress. This expectation is a part of human resource management. Herzberg's research tells us that an appealing work environment does not meet the worker's expectation; dissatisfaction is usually evident.

Employee Health Concerns and Complaints

Employee concerns about the possibility of health problems resulting from regular user interface with technology, raw materials and/or production processes focus on the following areas:

1.

2.

3.

4.

5.

RSI is the acronym for . . .

Visual dysfunction includes visual distress from conditions such as:

1.

2.

3.

4.

5.

Research indicates the above visual distress conditions appear to be caused by . . .

- poor design of visual display terminals;
- poor design of the physical environment; and
- long, intensive work intervals without adequate rest periods. No research to confirm computer workers have higher rates of distress than other workers.

CTS stands for . . .

Musculoskeletal problems describe complaints or discomfort primarily occurring in body parts such as:

1.

2.

3.

4.

5.

Tendinitis is . . .

Two types of emotional disturbances have affected employees' abilities to perform specific business functions. Give examples of each.

Mood disturbances

1.

2.

3.

4.

5.

Psychosomatic disorders

1.

2.

3.

4.

5.

Psychosocial disturbances focus on specific problems relating to the work environment. Give examples of these:

1.

2.

3.

4.

Responsibility for Health and Safety

Name some of the ways an organization may gain through health and safety programs:

1.

2.

3.

4.

5.

6.

What does **OSHA** stand for?

What are its provisions?

1.

2.

3.

Workers' compensation laws provide benefits for injured workers or their dependents. State the provisions of these laws:

1.

2.

3.

4.

5.

Employee Assistance Programs (EAPs) provide help for what type of situations?

1.

2.

3.

Stress

Stress is inevitable--as is change--both on the job and in personal life.

Stressors are the stimuli that induce stress.

Stress can have physical or psychological expressions, or both. Stress involves an excessive amount of strain. The amount of strain deemed "excessive" varies with the individual and with the organization.

Stress can have positive effects. Some of these positive effects are:

Eustress (instress) is referred to as ( ) positive ( ) negative stress.

The negative effects of stress include:

1.

2.

3.

101

4.

5.

Two conditions required for possible stress to become actual stress are:

1.

2.

The Cycle of Stress

Dr. Hans Seyle, the father of stress studies, indicates that everyone has a basic stress threshold. He has developed a cycle known as the General Adaptation Syndrome (GAS). Explain the three stages of this cycle:

Stage I:

Stage II:

Stage III:

Causes of Stress

The three general categories of the causes of stress are:

1.

2.

3.

Open office layouts can create more ( ) eustress ( ) distress than traditional designs. Private offices with pleasant views may lead to ( ) eustress or ( ) distress.

The two primary types of interpersonal demands among people within organizational settings which can be very stressful are:

1.

2.

Common environmental stressors include:

1.

2.

3.

4.

5.

Common personal causes of stress include:

1.

2.

3.

4.

Stress as an Additive Phenomenon

Explain the expression, "the last straw."

Manifestations of Stress

Shifts in behavior that are largely attributable to stress-related causes include changes in:

1.

2.

3.

4.

5.

6.

7.

103

Changes in a person's medical condition may produce physical or physiological symptoms that seem to be primarily stress related. These may include:

1.

2.

3.

4.

5.

6.

Emotional or psychological symptoms in a person's mental well-being that seem to be primarily stress-related may indicate increase in:

1.

2.

3.

4.

5.

6.

Changes in behavior and relationships on the job which may be indicative of stress are:

1.

2.

3.

4.

5.

6.

7.

8.

Burnout is an ultimate result of stress and occurs when an individual . . .

- feels too much pressure
- does not have enough sources of satisfaction
- has decreased escape mechanisms

Stress Management Techniques

Stress reduction and management techniques include:

1.

2.

3.

4.

Organizations can support their employees and try to assist in stress management. However, unless the individual wants to improve, no single technique will work. Some activities the employee may try are:

1.

2.

3.

4.

5.

CHAPTER 9: EMPLOYEE SAFETY, HEALTH, AND STRESS

Additional Comments

Use this page to record terms and definitions you want to concentrate on, or to record additional information you have located from other resources.

CHAPTER 9: EMPLOYEE SAFETY, HEALTH, AND STRESS

Additional Comments

Use this page to record information found in readings, notes from lectures, or notes to yourself about topics to be researched.

CHAPTER 9: EMPLOYEE SAFETY, HEALTH, AND STRESS

Additional Comments

CHAPTER 10: PERFORMANCE APPRAISAL

In an effort to maintain top performing employees, organizations should have a regular process in place to evaluate employees. Evaluation is intended to determine strengths, weaknesses, areas where training is needed, and the ability to be promoted.

The Employee Evaluation Process

Standards must be in place to measure performance. The appraisal interview itself should be used as an informational motivational tool for both employers and employees.

Both the supervisor and employee should sign the appraisal documentation. The employee ( ) should ( ) should not be given the opportunity to write an explanatory statement for the personnel record if disagreement occurs over the appraisal statements.

Primary reasons for conducting performance appraisals on a regular basis are:

1.

2.

3.

4.

Types of Performance Appraisal Systems

Briefly describe each of the more common performance appraisal methods shown below:

Essay appraisal

Graphic rating scales

Checklist

Forced-choice rating

Critical incident

Ranking

Management by Objectives (MBO)

Managers should be trained to be consistent in their interviewing techniques used in connection with performance appraisals.

Problems in Employee Performance Appraisals

Common problems involved with conducting quality performance evaluation meetings include:

1.

2.

3.

4.

5.

6.

CHAPTER 10: PERFORMANCE APPRAISAL

Additional Comments

Use this page to record terms and definitions you want to concentrate on, or to record additional information you have located from other resources.

CHAPTER 10:   PERFORMANCE APPRAISAL

Additional Comments

Use this page to record information found in readings, notes from lectures, or notes to yourself about topics to be researched.

CHAPTER 10: PERFORMANCE APPRAISAL

Additional Comments

CHAPTER 11:   EMPLOYEE-LABOR RELATIONS

With the increasing amount of attention given to the concept of empowerment, more organizations are realizing the potential for market growth where employees are invited to offer suggestions and participate in the decision-making process and where employees listen to those suggestions.

Major Legislation Affecting Employee-Labor Relations

There are a number of significant federal labor relations laws which influence employee-employer relations and collective bargaining. Identify these laws and make statements about the major provisions of each.

1.

Provisions:

2.

Provisions:

3.

Provisions:

4.

Provisions:

Union-Management Relations

Name some occupational areas where unions are not dominant.

The National Labor Relations Act (1935) prohibits . . .

The work contrast resulting from collective bargaining will identify and explain such elements as:

1.

2.

3.

4.

5.

A successful work agreement is one bargained in good faith and is equitable to both parties--employees and their employer.

With or without unions, competitive companies need to respond to such questions as the following in order to provide fairness to all concerned:

1.

2.

3.

4.

5.

The number of persons belonging to labor unions now represents only about 16 percent of the total work force.

Employee Participation Systems

When an employer has focused more on productivity than people (employees), the results may be seen in one or all of the following behaviors:

1.

2.

3.

The key to an effective employee suggestion system is ...

Industrial psychologists have long advocated theories of motivation and employee motivators. Abraham Maslow (1960) and his Hierachy of Needs suggest that people have five stages of needs, ranging from survival to self-satisfaction. Motivators are also recognized as being situational.

Elements which some theorists say may invoke motivation on the employee's part are:

1.

2.

3.

CHAPTER 11: EMPLOYEE-LABOR RELATIONS

Additional Comments

Use this page to record terms and definitions you want to concentrate on, or to record additional information you have located from other resources.

CHAPTER 11: EMPLOYEE-LABOR RELATIONS

Additional Comments

Use this page to record information found in readings, notes from lectures, or notes to yourself about topics to be researched.

CHAPTER 11:   EMPLOYEE-LABOR RELATIONS

Additional Comments

CHAPTER 12:   GRIEVANCES, DISCIPLINE, AND COUNSELING

The processing of grievances is very time consuming, both in a union and in a nonunion environment. This process is of great interest to the average worker. Counseling is a part of the grievance process.

Discipline

It is necessary that every organization has in place a disciplinary process.

Discipline is typically defined as . . .

Administration of Discipline

Consistency is the key in the interpretation of rules and people treatment.

Progressive discipline involves . . .

The steps in progressive discipline as discussed in your text include:

1.

2.

3.

4.

5.

The goal of progressive discipline is not dismissal but rather an attempt to show the employee that basic procedures and policies must be respected.

Discipline without punishment typically includes the following steps:

1.

2.

3.

4.

Counseling is . . .

Coaching is . . .

Grievances in Nonunionized Settings

Among the methods for handling employee grievances in a nonunionized workplace are the following:

1.

2.

3.

4.

Grievances in Unionized Settings

In the union environment, the grievance process is spelled out in the _____ _____.
The steps in this process are:

1.

2.

3.

4.

Grievance Impasse Resolution Methods

Describe the following methods used to resolve grievances:

Fact-finding

Conciliation

Mediation

Arbitration

CHAPTER 12:   GRIEVANCES, DISCIPLINE, AND COUNSELING

Additional Comments

Use this page to record terms and definitions you want to concentrate on, or to record additional information you have located from other resources.

CHAPTER 12:   GRIEVANCES, DISCIPLINE, AND COUNSELING

Additional Comments

Use this page to record information found in readings, notes from lectures, or notes to yourself about topics to be researched.

CHAPTER 12: GRIEVANCES, DISCIPLINE, AND COUNSELING

Additional Comments

CHAPTER 13: EMPLOYEE SEPARATION PROCESSES

A difficult part of the employment process is the separation of people from their workplace. This decision may be voluntary or involuntary on the part of the employee.

Separation

The four types of employment separations experienced by employees are:

1.

2.

3.

4.

Responsibility for Separation

The purpose of an exit interview is to . . .

Legal Separations

"Employment-at-will" means . . .

If the separation is involuntary, organizations may be required to do the following:

1.

2.

3.

4.

Documentation of Separations

Records should be maintained on former employees as well as existing and potential employees. Types of information to be maintained include:

1.

2.

3.

4.

Managers should be trained in the appropriate way to process terminations.

CHAPTER 13:   EMPLOYEE SEPARATION PROCESSES

Additional Comments

Use this page to record terms and definitions you want to concentrate on, or to record additional information you have located from other resources.

CHAPTER 13: EMPLOYEE SEPARATION PROCESSES

Additional Comments

Use this page to record information found in readings, notes from lectures, or notes to yourself about topics to be researched.

CHAPTER 13:   EMPLOYEE SEPARATION PROCESSES

Additional Comments

CHAPTER 14:   PRINCIPLES AND THEORIES OF MANAGEMENT

Management is the process of getting things done through other people.   Management is the development of the work environment in which people can accomplish organizational and personal goals efficiently and effectively.   The field of management is based on specific principles and theories, which form a historical background for the field.

Classical Management Theories

The three classical management theories are:

1.

2.

3.

The four theorists who contributed the most to the study of scientific management are:

1.

2.

3.

4.

The **"father of scientific management"** is...

The focus of scientific management was on...

Frederick Taylor's four principles, as applied to tasks and jobs, include:

1.

2.

3.

4.

Taylor's primary belief was that workers performing the same job should be using...

Lillian and Frank Gilbreth were well known for their work in _____
_____ and _____ _____.

The three basic elements included in their analyses are:

1.

2.

3.

A **therblig** is...

Henry L. Gantt was concerned with the _____ side of scientific management. His two principles focused on human behavior are:

1.

2.

Gantt is probably best known for developing the _____ _____.

William H. Leffingwell is known as the **"father of office management."** Leffingwell authored the book, _____, which contains principles still important to today's secretaries and office personnel.

His five steps to office management are:

1.

2.

3.

4.

5.

Administrative management is defined as the application of the functions of planning, organizing, activating, and controlling the administration at the upper levels of management within an organization. Administrative theory is based on the following four principles:

1.

2.

3.

4.

Henri Fayol, a management theorist, is considered the **"father of administrative management."** Fayol's general theory included three types of information. These three types are:

1.

2.

3.

Technical, commercial, financial, and managerial activities are examples of _____ type of information, according to Fayol.

Fayol identified 14 general principles of management which could be applied to management in any organization. Explain each of these general principles listed below:

Division of work

133

Authority and responsibility

Discipline

Unity of command

Unity of direction

Subordination of individual interest to general interest

Renumeration of personnel

Centralization

Scalar chain

Order

Equity

Stability of tenure of personnel

Initiative

134

Espirit de corp

The acceptance theory of authority states that...

Chester Barnard maintained that executive (administrative) management consisted of several key functions. Name and explain these key functions.

Explain the **bureaucratic theory** as developed and defined by Max Weber:

Human Resource Management Theory

The four principles of human relations theory outlined in your text are:

1 .

2 .

3 .

4 .

Explain the **Hawthorn studies** conducted by **Elton Mayo and Fritz Roethlisberger**.

The four basic needs crucial to all humans and which should be recognized by management are:

1 .

2 .

3 .

4 .

Mary Parker Follett introduced a concept known as the law of the _____. This law suggests that leadership effectiveness is primarily a result of an active interaction and interrelationship of three sets of factors. These three factors are:

1 .

2 .

3 .

Two other notable processes attributed to Follett are:

1 .

2.

Several human relations and behavioral theorists have been introduced in this book. Give a brief description of the work of those listed below:

Douglas McGregor

Abraham Maslow

Rensis Likert

Frederick Herzberg

Name and explain each of the five components of the open systems theory in organizations:

1.

2.

3.

4.

137

5.

Theory Z is based on...

Management Science Theory

Name and make a statement about each of the three areas within management science theory:

1.

2.

3.

Total Quality Management

The **production era** could be described as...

The **marketing era** could be described as...

The **total marketing concep**t could be described as...

The **quality control era** could be described as...

Philip Crosby, a leading authority on quality, focuses on four absolutes of quality. These are:

1 .

2 .

3 .

4 .

According to Crosby, the five problems that often arise in trying to attain quality are:

1 .

2 .

3 .

4 .

5 .

W. Edwards Deming is recognized worldwide for his contributions to the quality movement. Deming's absolutes of quality included 14 rules regarding the achievement and maintenance of quality within any organization. Explain these 14 rules:

Creating constancy of purpose

Adopting a new philosophy

Inspecting products or services continuously

Awarding contracts for quality service

Improving the production of goods or services

Providing training and retraining

Instituting leadership

Eliminating fear of innovation

Fostering teamwork

Eliminating useless slogans and targets

140

Eliminating numerical performance quotas

Developing pride of workmanship

Providing training in TQM approaches

Taking managerial action to make changes

Along with these basic rules for the TQM process, Deming identified seven major barriers to effective implementation of the process. These barriers are:

1.

2.

3.

4.

5.

6.

7.

The basic premises of **TQM** are:

1.

2.

3.

CHAPTER 14:   PRINCIPLES AND THEORIES OF MANAGEMENT

Additional Comments

Use this page to record terms and definitions you want to concentrate on, or to record additional information you have located from other resources.

143

CHAPTER 14:   PRINCIPLES AND THEORIES OF MANAGEMENT

Additional Comments

Use this page to record information found in readings, notes from lectures, or notes to yourself about topics to be researched.

CHAPTER 14: PRINCIPLES AND THEORIES OF MANAGEMENT

Additional Comments

CHAPTER 15: DECISION-MAKING PROCESSES

Most decisions are made in an atmosphere of uncertainty, risk, time pressure, imperfect information, and a lack of knowledge as to responses. Decision making is a part of all management functions: planning, organizing, leading, and controlling and is made at all levels of an organization by both managers and nonmanagers. All persons make decisions constantly both in their professional and personal lives. Decision making is a critical responsibility.

Organizational Decision Making

Managers who are "left-brain thinkers" tend to arrive at _____ and _____ situations and perhaps are stronger advocates of classical theory.

The classical model is considered the ( ) normative ( ) behavioral model because it defines how a particular decision maker should make decisions.

The ( ) behavioral ( ) classical model describes how managers actually make decisions in business situations.

The behavioral (administrative) model is based on the work of Herbert Simon and incorporates two basic concepts. Name and define the two basic concepts of this model:

1.

2.

Describe the differences individuals experience in making personal and organizational decisions:

Personal decisions

Organizational decisions

146

Satisficing is defined as...

Optimizing refers to...

Logical Reasoning Process

The steps in the scientific approach to decision making are:

1 .

2 .

3 .

4 .

The reasons for failure to identify real causes include:

1 .

2 .

3 .

Brainstorming is...

Brainwriting is...

Operations research uses _____ _____ and techniques for analyzing complex decision problems.

147

Qualitative factors are described in terms of the certainty, uncertainty, limited certainty, or risk to be taken when alternatives to problems are considered. Explain each of these terms:

Certainty

Uncertainty

Limited certainty

Risk

Helpful analytical tools for decision making include:

1 .

2 .

3 .

Vroom and Yetton are associated with the _____ method of decision making.

DDS stand for...

Three parts of a DDS that are of most help to a manager in the decision-making process are:

1 .

2 .

3 .

CHAPTER 15:   DECISION-MAKING PROCESSES

Additional Comments

Use this page to record terms and definitions you want to concentrate on, or to record additional information you have located from other resources.

CHAPTER 15: DECISION-MAKING PROCESSES

Additional Comments

Use this page to record information found in readings, notes from lectures, or notes to yourself about topics to be researched.

CHAPTER 15:   DECISION-MAKING PROCESSES

Additional Comments

CHAPTER 16: THE FUNCTIONS OF MANAGEMENT

Management is the process of achieving organizational objectives through the use of people and other resources. All managers must perform the functions of management: planning, organizing, leading, and controlling. Communication is the underlying foundation of all of the management functions.

The most important resource for any manager is the human resource. It is the people who will make an operation successful or unsuccessful. The effective manager learns how to mix the functions of management to match the mix of people.

Planning

Planning is the most important and basic management function. Planning involves:

1.

and

2.

The purpose of planning is to...

The five most important components of planning are:

1.

2.

3.

4.

5.

The _____ is the basic purpose for an organization's existence.

The term **objective** refers to...

Short-term goals or objectives control _____ plans. **Long-term goals** or objectives are usually plans for the future--usually ____ to ____ years.

152

Peter Drucker identified eight key areas in which any organization should have specific objectives. Drucker's objectives are:

1 .

2 .

3 .

4 .

5 .

6 .

7 .

8 .

Strategy describes the way a manager or planner intends to use the organization's

_____.

A ( ) policy ( ) procedure describes actions or decisions appropriate to particular situations.

A ( ) policy ( ) procedure describes a set or sequence of steps to be followed in performing a specific task or action.

A **rule** states...

Plans are usually developed by management for four specific time periods and degrees of specificity. Name and define these time periods:

1 .

2 .

3 .

4 .

State the difference between the two basic types of plans referred to in your text:

1.

2.

The purpose of planning is...

MBO means...

Limitations with the use of MBO include:

1.

2.

3.

4.

5.

Organizing

Organizing allows a group to operate and function effectively. Organizing becomes necessary as a result of planning.

The organization process involves:

- the identification of major activities;

- the division of major activities into horizontal groupings;

- the vertical division into horizontal groupings;

- the assignment of authority to groupings; and

- the designing of jobs.

154

The principles of organization have developed over time. Define each of the principles listed below.

Unity of command

Chain of command

Span of control

Departmentation

Commensurate authority

The exception principle

Authority is...

Responsibility is....

Line authority is ( ) direct ( ) indirect authority which carries with it the right to give orders and have decisions implemented.

Staff authority is supportive in nature. It ( ) does ( ) does not give the right to command.

The three types of staff are:

1 .

2 .

3 .

155

The organization chart is a written or graphic representation of...

An organization manual will generally include job descriptions for positions shown on the organization chart along with written policies and procedures.

Leading

Leading or directing involves the ongoing process of guiding, coaching, and influencing other people's work performance toward the goals of the organization's mission.

The term _____ refers to a person who directs the work of one or more individuals at the first level of management.

Supervisors must represent the organization to the employees and the employees to the organization.

Routine duties of the supervisor include:

1.

2.

3.

4.

5.

6.

Determinants of effective supervisory behavior include:

1.

2.

3.

4.

5.

The informal leader is selected by the group. The informal leader can make the supervisor's role more or less difficult by influence with the group.   List positive/negative influences of the informal group upon the organization:

1.

2.

3.

4.

5.

6.

Name sources of informal power:

1.

2.

3.

4.

5.

Other sources of informal power come from association with other groups, experience, drive and determination, and education.

Make a statement about each of the reasons for resistance behavior which are listed below:

Loss of power and prestige

Fear of job elimination

157

Role ambiguity

Changed relationships

Changed work patterns

Productivity is...

Explain the difference between effectiveness and efficiency.

Effectiveness

and

Efficiency

Teamwork is often associated with _____. High morale tends to be accompanied by more pleasant work conditions, lower employee turnover, lower absenteeism, and less tardiness.

Controlling

Controlling focuses on evaluating performance according to the plans that have been established.

Controlling, although a part of each of the management functions, seems to be the most closely related to _____. Controlling is the process of:

1.

2.

3.

The four basic steps in the control process are:

1.

2.

3.

4.

When correction is necessary as a result of a gap between standards and actual performance, management may respond with these types of actions:

1.

2.

3.

One of the control mechanisms is feedforward measures. Give examples of this type of control:

Concurrent controls are also called _____ controls. Concurrent controls are important to have in place in order to minimize damage that may occur if precontrols fail.

Feedback controls are often known as _____ measures.

Effective control mechanisms must be:

1.

2.

3.

4.

Certain kinds of information that need to be controlled include:

1.

2.

3.

4.

5.

Specialized controls might include inventory control, quality control, and production control.

Explain the difference between **standard** and **standardization**:

Standard

Standardization

Standards may relate to time, materials, performance, reliability, appearance, or any quantifiable characteristic of the product or service.

A **quality** standard is...

Quality standards typically relate to:

1.

2.

3.

4.

Section III: Organizations and Management
Part III: Management, 1 Hour, 45 minutes
150 iitems, 45% of Part III

The type of quality control technique used depends on the phase of the production process--input, process, or outcome.   Give examples of controls for the three phases of production:

Input

Process

Outcome

A **budget** is...

Name and explain the difference between two types of costing:

Process costing

Job costing

Costs may be classified as direct costs, indirect costs, and semifixed costs. Give examples of each type of classification:

Direct costs

Indirect costs

Semifixed costs

The **Gantt chart**, the **critical path method** (CPM), and **program evaluation and review technique** (PERT) are specialized tools to improve the quality of control.

Some of the forms used for the Gantt chart are:

1 .

2 .

3 .

Gantt-type charts are the most widely used time control and analysis measures.

For projects to be charted using the PERT method, they must have the following characteristics:

1 .

2 .

3 .

4 .

The major advantage of PERT is that it forces managers to plan.

Both Gantt and PERT stress_____. The critical path method stresses _____.

The primary features of CPM are:

1 .

2 .

3 .

Computer applications have made the preparation and interpretation of PERT and CPM charts easier and more effective.

The principle of **management by exception** (MBE) focuses attention on...

162

When a manager implements the exception principle, the components of the delegation process will include the following:

1 .

2 .

3 .

State the justification for using the management by exception principle:

Communicating

Communication is the process of transmitting ideas in such a way that others will understand and be able to use the transmitted information.

Public relations policies are necessary for organizations to be responsive to the needs of customers or clients. These policies must be established so that:

1 .

2 .

3 .

Employee relations policies are designed to maintain good employee relations throughout the organization. These policies cover such activities as:

1 .

2 .

163

3.

4.

5.

6.

Meetings tend to be either formal or informal.   Both types of meetings provide the most prominent strategy used to communicate information. In-house meetings will generally fall into one of the categories listed below. Make statements about each category:

General meeting

Departmental meeting

Committee meeting

Explain the difference between the standing committee and the ad hoc committee:

Standing committee

Ad hoc committee

List the purposes for which meetings may be held:

1.

2.

3.

4.

5.

6.

7.

Some of the problems with meetings are:

Techniques managers can use to increase the likelihood that a meeting will be effective are:

1.

2.

3.

4.

5.

6.

Conflict can cause communication to deteriorate and people to become openly hostile toward each other. The goals of a meeting in which conflict occurs cannot be achieved effectively.   Name and make statements about the three types of conflict which may occur:

1.

2.

3.

Three basic steps used to resolve conflict are:

1.

2.

3.

166

Feedback is the reaction from the receiver to the sender regarding a communication sent. Feedback is a continuous process. The two basic types of feedback are direct and delayed. Make statements about each type.

Direct feedback

Delayed feedback

There are three levels of feedback. Feedback is expressed in different ways at each level. Give the characteristics for each level:

First level

Second level

Third level

Communication always involves at least two people--a sender and a receiver. Make statements about the directions of communication:

One-direction communication

Bidirectional communication

Multidirectional communication

Formal communication uses four communication channels that involve directional communication and the levels of feedback. Give examples of each of the communication channels:

Downward communication

Upward communication

Lateral communication

Diagonal communication

Feedback is vital to the communication process. The primary problem with feedback is that it is not often received when it is needed the most.   Make statements about each of the areas indicated below as they relate to feedback:

Delayed feedback

Information distortion

Information gap

Information overload

169

CHAPTER 16: THE FUNCTIONS OF MANAGEMENT

Additional Comments

Use this page to record terms and definitions you want to concentrate on, or to record additional information you have located from other resources.

CHAPTER 16: THE FUNCTIONS OF MANAGEMENT

Additional Comments

Use this page to record information found in readings, notes from lectures, or notes to yourself about topics to be researched.

CHAPTER 16:   THE FUNCTION OF MANAGEMENT

Additional Comments

CHAPTER 17: PRODUCTION MANAGEMENT

Production management is gaining international attention as competitiveness becomes more critical to our economy. The management strategies of our production competitors are being investigated as the trade center of the world is shifting.

There is a productive system in every enterprise--private or public, small or large, national or international, service-focused or product-focused.

The attention being given to production management is gaining in the overall visibility of organizations and has found its place alongside materials management concept and function.

Facilities

Four key questions to ask regarding "the right facility" are:

1.

2.

3.

4.

The right location is considered to be that location which will...

A product-focused organization is usually associated with _____-_____ operations. The work flow is organized entirely around the production of the product.

Determining the right spot for a function within a facility requires attempting to measure the _____ _____ existing among the units.

The amount of _____ allocated to a function is dependent on its importance in relation to the production of the firm's final product or service.

Make statements to outline the difference in the open and traditional office designs:

Open

Traditional

The most important requirement in designing efficient offices is _____.

Ergonomics is the study of...

Materials--Procurement, Processing, and Control

Materials often represent 20 to 30 percent of the total assets of a manufacturing firm.   Organizations consider the procurement, processing, and control of inventories a function often requiring daily control.

Effective inventory replenishment policies include the following four elements:

1.

2.

3.

4.

New businesses usually find it is ( ) more ( ) less cost effective to purchase most parts and components.

Three reasons inventories received from vendors need to be checked when received are:

1.

2.

3.

Inventory management is responsible for maintaining...

174

Effective inventory management policies allow the interdependent functions of _____,

_____, and _____ to be supplied with the right materials and components at the right time to meet schedules at the lowest costs.

EOQ stands for...

Lead time is...

Two basic types of inventories are:

1.

2.

Name three variables that may affect inventory management even though they are out of the firm's control:

1.

2.

3.

Distribution inventories are frequently ( ) more ( ) less difficult to manage because they are dependent on consumer wants and needs.

Name and explain two frequently used inventory control systems:

1.

2.

Methods and Quality Control

Quality generally means meeting specified standards. The measures of quality will differ among manufacturing and service systems.

Measures of quality in manufacturing systems can be related to:

1 .

2 .

3 .

Measures of quality in service systems are often not as objective as in manufacturing systems. Measures may relate to:

1 .

2 .

3 .

The functions are to:

1 .

2 .

Quality control involves:

1 .

2 .

3 .

4 .

Product warranty includes both that _____ by the manufacturer and that

_____ by the manufacturer that the product will be safe for consumer use.

Briefly describe the **quality control process**:

Quality control can occur at any one or all three of the production phases. These three phases are:

1 .

2 .

3 .

The techniques for controlling quality fall into three categories. Name these three categories and give examples of each.

Planning and Scheduling Production

Successful management of production requires control of costs by eliminating waste and operating at a high level of efficiency. Planning and scheduling production require making decisions that are responsive to such variables as:

1 .

2 .

3 .

Aggregate planning is a process involving:

1 .

2 .

3 .

Name aggregate planning methods available and give an example of each:

1 .

2 .

3 .

Two examples of network planning methods are **CPM** and **PERT**. Make a statement about each:

CPM

PERT

178

CHAPTER 17: PRODUCTION MANAGEMENT

Additional Comments

Use this page to record terms and definitions you want to concentrate on, or to record additional information you have located from other resources.

CHAPTER 17:   PRODUCTION MANAGEMENT

Additional Comments

Use this page to record information found in readings, notes from lectures, or notes to yourself about topics to be researched.

CHAPTER 17:   PRODUCTION MANAGEMENT

Additional Comments

CHAPTER 18: MARKETING MANAGEMENT

Marketing consists of the performance of business activities that direct the flow of goods and services from producer to consumer and user. Marketing management tries to match up goods and services with markets and to effect transfers in the ownership of these goods and services. Marketing and production activities are interlocked.

Firms with a marketing "attitude" believe that customer needs and their satisfaction are the guiding concerns of the business.

Marketing Policy

The "four P's" of marketing are:

P

P

P

P

In combination, the four P's make up what is known as the _____ _____.

Implementation of the Marketing Concept/Marketing Mix

Marketing management includes:

1.

2.

3.

4.

Complete the chart below by identifying marketing controllables and marketing uncontrollables.

Marketing Controllables	Marketing Uncontrollables
1.	1.
2.	2.
3.	3.
4.	4.
5.	5.
6.	6.

Potential buyers are separated into two categories. These categories are:

1.

2.

Describe the difference between these two categories:

The most common variables to consider when setting prices are:

1 .

2 .

3 .

Competition-oriented pricing implies that a major determinant for a firm's price decision is...

When price is set on **customer or demand-oriented pricing**, the price is set on the basis of...

The Clayton Act, as amended by the Robinson-Patman Act, prohibits the following pricing practices that discriminate among like purchasers:

1 .

2 .

3 .

4 .

A **marketing channel** is the path followed in the _____ or _____ transfer of the legal title to a product as it moves from producer to ultimate consumer or industrial user.

Transfer of title is ( ) direct ( ) indirect when the producer sells the product outright to a wholesaler or retailer.

Transfer of title is ( ) direct ( ) indirect when the agent (or middleperson) does not take title but simply negotiates its transfer to another middleperson.

Define and make statements about the following types of consumer goods channels:

Channel A

Channel B

Channel C

Channel D

Name the product characteristics for determining the appropriate distribution channel(s):

1.

2.

3.

4.

5.

The three major decision areas in **product promotion** are:

1.

2.

3.

The three product promotion areas constitute the **promotional mix.**

185

Advertising

Advertising, a form of promotion, is a nonpersonal sales message paid for by a company. This company is called the _____.

Advertising's most frequent assignment is to...

Advertising, depending on what is being promoted, can be classified into one of two categories:

1 .

2 .

Institutional advertising does not mention specific products and is most concerned with the following objectives:

1 .

2 .

3 .

4 .

Product advertising has as the primary purpose to make consumers buy a specific product or use a specific service. Product advertising can be used to:

1 .

2 .

3 .

4 .

5 .

Advertising media refers to...

186

Media selection is usually determined by:

1 .

2 .

The cost of advertising is based largely on:

1 .

2 .

3 .

List four things advertising **cannot** do:

1 .

2 .

3 .

4 .

Sales Analysis and Control

The primary purpose of sales analysis is to detect an organization's marketing _____ and
_____.

Name the primary types of sales analysis and what information each type can provide:

1 .

2 .

3 .

Market Analysis

Market analysis, or market research, is the systematic gathering, recording, and analyzing of data about marketing problems toward the goal of providing information useful in marketing decision making.

The two primary sources of data are internal and external sources. Define each:

Internal data sources

External data sources

Market research activities are involved primarily with finding facts in three areas. Name these three areas.

1.

2.

3.

Primary data sources for project planning are:

Secondary data sources for project planning include:

Name and explain the three main methods for collecting data:

1.

2.

3.

188

Three principal applications appropriate to the survey method are:

1.

2.

3.

Traffic Management

The total process of moving, handling, and storing goods on the way from the producer to the user is called physical distribution. Physical distribution includes both _____ and _____ of products.

Decisions on modes of transportation should be made with the goal of...

The time required for moving goods from warehouses to customers is called _____
_____.

Transportation decisions should be based on cost and transport-time considerations.

Name and explain the three types of carriers:

1.

2.

3.

The most important type of freight transportation in the United States is the _____.

Piggyback service refers to...

Fishyback service refers to...

189

The railroad's biggest competitor is the _____.

Among the oldest forms of transportation are _____ and _____.

Pipeline transportation is important as a major form of carrier for...

Air transportation is also big business and growing rapidly.

Special services available to shippers are listed below. Make a statement about each.

Overnight package express delivery

Electronic mail delivery

Parcel post

Consolidated delivery systems

Bus package services

Freight forwarders/freight consolidators

Outline trends in traffic management:

CHAPTER 18:   MARKETING MANAGEMENT

Additional Comments

Use this page to record terms and definitions you want to concentrate on, or to record additional information you have located from other resources.

CHAPTER 18: MARKETING MANAGEMENT

Additional Comments

Use this page to record information found in readings, notes from lectures, or notes to yourself about topics to be researched.

CPS® PLANNING FORM

e decided to become a Certified Professional Secretary®· Toward my goal, I will plan to sit for the
ination in: ( ) November   ( ) May, 19 ____.

preparation plan:

er: 1.   Application/requirements for CPS® examination available from PSI®, CPS ®Division.
              CPS® Outline and Bibliography available from PSI®, CPS® Division.
              (There is no charge for the application/requirements. There is a charge for the
              Outline and Bibliography)

              Note: As soon as this material is received, read it carefully. Highlight the postmark
              dates for filing application and supporting materials to qualify for the examination
              dates of your choice.

       2.   Resource Materials

              ( ) CPS® Review Modules
              ( ) Self-Study Guides – the CPS® Review Modules

              (These materials are available for sale from Prentice Hall Publishers.)

:   ( ) Join a noontime or informal study group.
       ( ) Commit to a study schedule.
       ( ) Outline a time frame for certification completion.
       ( ) Investigate local library resources.

on: ( ) Read resource materials.
       ( ) Read materials on study techniques and on taking tests.
       ( ) Take a Pre-Test to identify needs.
       ( ) Begin using this Self-Study Guide.

_____   _____
ture   Date

193

Study Tip Exam Prep (S.T.E.P.) Card
PART I: BEHAVIORAL SCIENCE

Mentally review these terms until you can define them quickly.

1. Aggression	26. Avoidance learning	51. Attitude	76. Valence
2. Type A	27. Hygiene factors	52. Synergy	77. Isolation
3. Nonverbal communication	28. Decoding	53. Role analysis	78. Noise
4. Paralanguage	29. Organization chart	54. Efficiency	79. Performing
5. Unfreezing	30. Ad hoc committee	55. Role conflict	80. Group think
6. Downsizing	31. Motion study	56. Goal	81. Behavior
7. Coaching	32. Informal group	57. Power need	82. Substitution
8. Empathy	33. Standing committee	58. Repression	83. Emotions
9. Message	34. Authoritarianism	59. Machiavellianism	84. Feelings
10. <---> communication	35. Acquired needs	60. Defense mechanisms	85. Planned change
11. Public distance	36. Self	61. Motivators	86. Communication process
12. Gangplank principle	37. Perception	62. Communication	87. Rationalization
13. Norming	38. Law of effect	63. Vertical communication	88. "Y" network
14. Quality circles	39. Rumor-mongering	64. Goals	89. Cooptation
15. Affiliation needs	40. Intrinsic rewards	65. Extinction	90. Frustration
16. Feedback	41. Storming	66. Self-fulfilling prophecy	91. Circle network
17. Projection	42. Reinforcement	67. Horn effect	92. Withdrawal
18. Informal communication	43. Need	68. Self-concept	93. Message channel
19. Active listening	44. Coping behavior	69. Extrinsic rewards	94. Motivation
20. OD	45. Formal group	70. Personality	95. Resignation
21. Performance gap	46. Role ambiguity	71. Traits	96. Effectiveness
22. Grapevine	47. Achievement needs	72. Isolation	97. Value system
23. Fixation	48. Halo effect	73. Pygmalion effect	98. Forming
24. Reactive change	49. Stereotyping	74. Refreezing	99. Change agent
25. 1 Communication	50. Assertiveness	75. Encoding	100. Semantics

Study Tip Exam Prep (S.T.E.P.) Card
PART I: BEHAVIORAL SCIENCE

Mentally review these terms until you can define them quickly.

1. Aggression	26. Avoidance learning	51. Attitude	76. Valence
2. Type A	27. Hygiene factors	52. Synergy	77. Isolation
3. Nonverbal communication	28. Decoding	53. Role analysis	78. Noise
4. Paralanguage	29. Organization chart	54. Efficiency	79. Performing
5. Unfreezing	30. Ad hoc committee	55. Role conflict	80. Group think
6. Downsizing	31. Motion study	56. Goal	81. Behavior
7. Coaching	32. Informal group	57. Power need	82. Substitution
8. Empathy	33. Standing committee	58. Repression	83. Emotions
9. Message	34. Authoritarianism	59. Machiavellianism	84. Feelings
10. <---> communication	35. Acquired needs	60. Defense mechanisms	85. Planned change
11. Public distance	36. Self	61. Motivators	86. Communication process
12. Gangplank principle	37. Perception	62. Communication	87. Rationalization
13. Norming	38. Law of effect	63. Vertical communication	88. "Y" network
14. Quality circles	39. Rumor-mongering	64. Goals	89. Cooptation
15. Affiliation needs	40. Intrinsic rewards	65. Extinction	90. Frustration
16. Feedback	41. Storming	66. Self-fulfilling prophecy	91. Circle network
17. Projection	42. Reinforcement	67. Horn effect	92. Withdrawal
18. Informal communication	43. Need	68. Self-concept	93. Message channel
19. Active listening	44. Coping behavior	69. Extrinsic rewards	94. Motivation
20. OD	45. Formal group	70. Personality	95. Resignation
21. Performance gap	46. Role ambiguity	71. Traits	96. Effectiveness
22. Grapevine	47. Achievement needs	72. Isolation	97. Value system
23. Fixation	48. Halo effect	73. Pygmalion effect	98. Forming
24. Reactive change	49. Stereotyping	74. Refreezing	99. Change agent
25. 1 Communication	50. Assertiveness	75. Encoding	100. Semantics

1

THEORY Y

2

COMMUNICATION CHANNELS

+ +

3

COMMUNICATION BARRIERS

4

ORGANIZATIONAL CHANGE

+ +

5

COMPONENTS OF A
FORMAL GROUP

6

FEEDBACK
(in the communication process)

2

Communication Channels are:

1. One-on-one (verbal);
2. Written;
3. Non-verbal;
4. Telephone; and
5. Automated processes.

1

Characteristics of Theory Y

1. Attitudinal position of leaders
   developed by McGregor
2. Assumptions:
   - Most people like and value work.
   - Most people seek responsibility.
   - People should be encouraged to be creative.
   - People should focus on self-actualization.

4

Three primary areas of organizational change:

1. Technological
2. Structural
3. Behavioral

3

Factors (internal/external to the individual) that prevent the sender's message from being received with the intended understanding. Barriers may include:

1. Terminology and
2. Cultural differences.

6

Feedback is:

1. Critical to improving the quality of
   communication; and
2. The opportunity for clarifying message
   content, personal emotions,
   incomplete information.

5

Components of a formal group are:

1. Leader;
2. Goals;
3. Members; and
4. Work arrangement.

7

TYPES OF INFORMAL GROUPS

8

COPING BEHAVIORS

9

AGGRESSION

10

ACTIVE COPING
DEFENSE MECHANISMS

11

ISOLATION

12

REGRESSION

8

Three types of coping behaviors are:

1. Trial and error;
2. Reshaping the problem; and
3. Revising the goal.

7

Types of informal groups include:

1. Task;
2. Project;
3. Committees; and
4. Training (T-group).

10

Active coping defense mechanisms:

Aggression   Fixation

Rationalization   Substitution

Rumor-mongering   Projection

Conscience hypocrisy

9

Agression

1. Active coping mechanism/response to frustration.
2. Behavior may be directed toward a person, inanimate object, or a situation.

12

Regression

1. Passive coping mechanism/response to frustration
2. Desire to escape the feelings of insecurity and stress to the safety of earlier role behaviors

11

Isolation

1. Passive coping mechanism/response to frustration
2. Desire to avoid stress
3. Behavior (detached, aloof) indicates desire to separate self from the situation.

13   14

DOUGLAS MCGREGOR   PASSIVE COPING
                               DEFENSE MECHANISMS

+ +

15   16

THEORY X   GRAPEVINE

+ +

17   18

ORGANIZATIONAL   HALO EFFECT
DEVELOPMENT (OD)

14

Passive coping defense mechanisms:

1. Resignation
2. Withdrawal
3. Isolation
4. Regression

13

Douglas McGregor

- Theorist
- Developed the THEORY X and THEORY Y approach to leadership

16

Grapevine:

The communication network

The informal network can carry both "planted" and "rumored" information.

15

THEORY X

1. Additional position of leaders developed by McGregor
2. Assumptions:
   - Most people dislike work.
   - Most people avoid responsibility.
   - Most people have security as dominant motivator.
   - Controls, threats, punishments are required for productivity.

18

Halo effect:

A term applied to situations where good qualities are attributed to a person without actual evidence of the quality.

17

OD is a:

1. Planned process for managing organizational change;
2. Proactive approach to change; and
3. Process through either an identified change agent or a work group.

19

CHANGE MODEL

20

THE MANAGERIAL GRID

21

LAW OF EFFECT

22

COPING MECHANISMS

23

MASLOW'S HEIRACHY OF NEEDS

24

HERZBERG'S TWO-FACTOR THEORY

20

Managerial grid:
1. A model developed by Blake and Mouton;
2. Portrays multiple leadership styles; and
3. Emphasizes concerns for production and people.

19

Change model involves three processes:
1. *Unfreezing* behaviors and attitudes--removal of present conditions;
2. *Moving*--introduces new behaviors and reinforcedments; and
3. *Refreezing*--rewards new behaviors.

22

Coping mechanisms:
1. Behaviors found in well-adjusted individuals to "live with" ineffective emotional responses
2. Active or passive responses
3. Responses believed to be more often an unconscious than a conscious behavior.

21

Law of effect:
1. Behavioral
2. Particular performance producing success
3. Experience of success results in repeated behavior by the individual

24

Herzberg two-factor theory:

Hygiene Factors
  Factors relating to the environment of the work place.

Motivational Factors
  Factors relating to the nature of the work itself.

23

25

McCLELLAND'S HIGHER LEVEL
NEEDS THEORY

26

COMMUNICATION MODEL

27

MOTIVATION PROCESS MODEL

28

ACTIVE LISTENING

29

INTRINSIC GOALS/REWARDS

30

EXTRINSIC GOALS/REWARDS

26

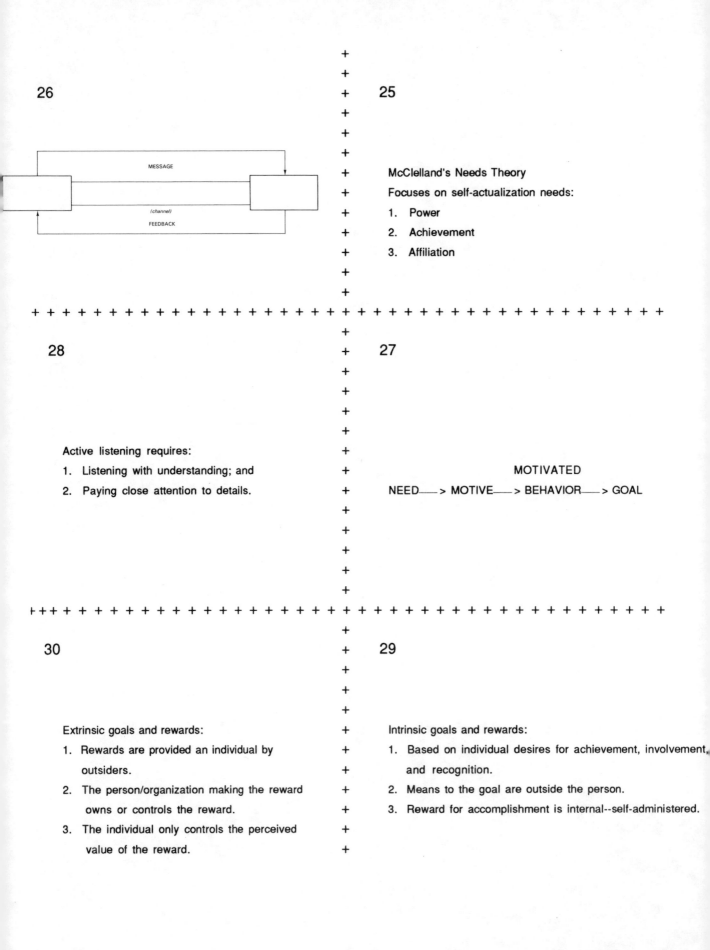

MESSAGE

(channel)

FEEDBACK

25

McClelland's Needs Theory

Focuses on self-actualization needs:

1. Power
2. Achievement
3. Affiliation

+ +

28

Active listening requires:

1. Listening with understanding; and
2. Paying close attention to details.

27

MOTIVATED

NEED——> MOTIVE——> BEHAVIOR——> GOAL

+ +

30

Extrinsic goals and rewards:

1. Rewards are provided an individual by outsiders.
2. The person/organization making the reward owns or controls the reward.
3. The individual only controls the perceived value of the reward.

29

Intrinsic goals and rewards:

1. Based on individual desires for achievement, involvement, and recognition.
2. Means to the goal are outside the person.
3. Reward for accomplishment is internal--self-administered.

Study Tip Exam Prep (S.T.E.P.) Card
PART II: HUMAN RESOURCE MANAGEMENT

Mentally review these terms until you can define them quickly.

1. BFOQ	26. Job specification	51. Recruitment	76. Structured Interview
2. Unstuctured interview	27. MTM	52. Internal recruiting	77. ERISA
3. Simulation	28. Mentor	53. Monetary rewards	78. Andragogy
4. OJT	29. Cognitive domain	54. Stress	79. Hypertension
5. Coaching	30. Conditioned stimulus	55. Mediation	80. GAS
6. Evaluation	31. Apprenticeship	56. Discipline	81. Exit interview
7. Learning curve	32. Burnout	57. Demotion	82. Ranking
8. Psychomotor domain	33. OSHA	58. Outplacement counseling	83. Essay appraisal
9. Job analysis	34. Visual dysfunction	59. Progressive discipline	84. Forced choice rating
10. Unconditioned stimulus	35. Musculoskeletal problems	60. Basic knowledge	85. Behavior
11. Pedagogy	36. Eustress	61. Employment-at-will	86. Output-based salary
12. EOE	37. Landrum-Griffin Act	62. Direct compensation	87. Yellow dog contracts
13. Internship	38. Featherbedding	63. Lectures	88. National Labor Relations Act
14. Development	39. Grievance	64. CAI	89. Learning domains
15. Sensitivity training	40. Probation	65. Nonmonetary incentives	90. Synthesis
16. Operant conditioning	41. Norris-LaGuardia Act	66. Bloom's taxonomy	91. Counseling
17. Job description	42. Performance standard	67. In-basket	92. Suggestion system
18. Affective domain	43. Discharge	68. Right-to-work law	93. Case method
19. Role-playing	44. Arbitration	69. Downsizing	94. MBO
20. Classical conditioning	45. Distress	70. Termination	95. Evaluation interview
21. Equal Pay Act	46. Wagner Act	71. Open-dooor policy	96. Layoff
22. Peter Principle	47. EAP	72. Taft-Hartley Act	97. Enstress
23. Asymptote	48. Stressor	73. Needs analysis	98. Job rotation
24. Title VII, Civil Rights Act	49. Training	74. Vesting	99. Equal Pay Act
25. Task analysis	50. Fair Labor Standards Act	75. Job evaluation	100. Learner readiness

Study Tip Exam Prep (S.T.E.P.) Card
PART II: HUMAN RESOURCE MANAGEMENT

Mentally review these terms until you can define them quickly.

1. BFOQ	26. Job specification	51. Recruitment	76. Structured Interview
2. Unstuctured interview	27. MTM	52. Internal recruiting	77. ERISA
3. Simulation	28. Mentor	53. Monetary rewards	78. Andragogy
4. OJT	29. Cognitive domain	54. Stress	79. Hypertension
5. Coaching	30. Conditioned stimulus	55. Mediation	80. GAS
6. Evaluation	31. Apprenticeship	56. Discipline	81. Exit interview
7. Learning curve	32. Burnout	57. Demotion	82. Ranking
8. Psychomotor domain	33. OSHA	58. Outplacement counseling	83. Essay appraisal
9. Job analysis	34. Visual dysfunction	59. Progressive discipline	84. Forced choice rating
10. Unconditioned stiimulus	35. Musculoskeletal problems	60. Basic knowledge	85. Behavior
11. Pedagogy	36. Eustress	61. Employment-at-will	86. Output-based salary
12. EOE	37. Landrum-Griffin Act	62. Direct compensation	87. Yellow dog contracts
13. Internship	38. Featherbedding	63. Lectures	88. National Labor Relations Act
14. Development	39. Grievance	64. CAI	89. Learning domains
15. Sensitivity training	40. Probation	65. Nonmonetary incentives	90. Synthesis
16. Operant conditioning	41. Norris-LaGuardia Act	66. Bloom's taxonomy	91. Counseling
17. Job description	42. Performance standard	67. In-basket	92. Suggestion system
18. Affective domain	43. Discharge	68. Right-to-work law	93. Case method
19. Role-playing	44. Arbitration	69. Downsizing	94. MBO
20. Classical conditioning	45. Distress	70. Termination	95. Evaluation interview
21. Equal Pay Act	46. Wagner Act	71. Open-dooor policy	96. Layoff
22. Peter Principle	47. EAP	72. Taft-Hartley Act	97. Enstress
23. Asymptote	48. Stressor	73. Needs analysis	98. Job rotation
24. Title VII, Civil Rights Act	49. Training	74. Vesting	99. Equal Pay Act
25. Task analysis	50. Fair Labor Standards Act	75. Job evaluation	100. Learner readiness

1

JOB ANALYSIS FORMULA

2

JOB EVALUATION

+ +

3

COMPENSATION PLANS

4

AGE DISCRIMINATION ACT (1967)

+ + + ++ +

5

INDIRECT COMPENSATION
(REQUIRED BY LAW)

6

INDIRECT COMPENSATION
(NOT REQUIRED BY LAW)

2

Job evaluation includes such factors as:

1. Skill requirement factors;
2. Effort requirement factors; and
3. Working condition factors.

1

Job Analysis Formula JA=JD+JS

Job analysis = job description + job specifications

4

Age Discrimination Act (1967) is legislation that: Prohibits employers with fifteen or more employees from implementing personnel practices that discriminate on the basis of race, color, sex, national origin, or religion.

3

The two basic types of compensation plans are:

1. Direct; and
2. Indirect.

6

Examples of indirect compensation not required by law are:

- Health insurance/group life;
- Paid vacations/birthdays off with pay;
- Profit sharing programs/stock options;
- Retirement programs;
- Employee discounts/company services;
- Bonuses; and
- Educational assistance.

5

Examples of indirect compensation required by state and federal laws are:

- Social security;
- Unemployment compensation payments;
- Workers' compensation; and
- Disability insurance.

7

CLASSICAL CONDITIONING

8

BASIC LEARNING APPROACHES

9

BASIC LEARNING STYLES

10

MANDATORY RETIREMENT ACT(1974)

11

THE LAW OF EFFECT

12

TYPES OF REINFORCEMENT

8

Two basic approaches to learning are:
1. Pedagogy (children); and
2. Andragogy (adults and nontraditional students).

7

Classical conditioning:
• Discovered by Ivan Pavlov;
• Learning as a stimulus response
• Passive way of learning

10

The Mandatory Retirement Act is legislation that:

Prohibits organizations from enforcing mandatory retirement before the age of seventy (70).

9

Basic styles of learning are categorized by:
• Concrete experience;
• Reflective observation;
• Abstract conceptualization; and
• Active experimentation.

12

The primary types of reinforcement are:
1. Continuous; and
2. Intermittent.

11

The *Law of Effect* states that behaviors that are rewarded tend to be repeated, while behaviors that go unnoticed or punished tend to cease.

13

OPTIONAL INDIRECT COMPENSATION

14

PRECONDITIONS FOR LEARNING

+ +

15

MOOD DISTURBANCES

16

PREGNANCY DISCRIMINATION ACT
(1978)

+ +

17

THEORIES OF LEARNING

18

APPLICANT SELECTION METHODS

14

Preconditions for learning include:
- Learner readiness
- Learner motivation

13

Examples of types of optional indirect compensation are:
- Extra payments for time worked
- Nonproduction awards and bonuses
- Payments for time not worked
- Payments for employee security
- Employee assistance programs

16

The pregnancy Discrimination Act is legislation that:
Prohibits firms from dismissing women sole on the basis of pregnancy and protects their job security during maternity leave.

15

Typical mood disturbances that employees indicate experiencing include:
- Anger
- Frustration
- Irritability
- Anxiety
- Depression

18

Common applicant selection methods include:
1. Screening applicants;
2. Employing testing;
3. Personal Interviews;
4. Matching organizational and individual goals;
5. Objectivity versus subjectivity.

17

The most common formal learning theories include:
- Classical conditioning
- Operant conditioning
- Social learning
- Cognitive learning

19   +   20
                                      +
                                      +
                                      +
                                      +
                                      +
                                      +
            STRESSOR   +   DOMAINS OF LEARNING
                                      +
                                      +
                                      +
                                      +
+ +
                                      +
21   +   22
                                      +
                                      +
                                      +
                                      +
                                      +
                                      +
        CAUSES OF STRESS   +   BURNOUT
                                      +
                                      +
                                      +
                                      +
                                      +
                                      +
+ +
                                      +
23   +   24
                                      +
                                      +
                                      +
                                      +
                                      +
      EQUAL PAY ACT (1963)   +   WAGE AND SALARY ADMINISTRATION
                                      +
                                      +
                                      +
                                      +
                                      +

20

The three domains of learning are:
- Cognitive domain
- Affective domain
- Psychomotor domain

19

Stressors are external stimuli or factors that may have external sources but may be generated through internal means.

22

Burnout is an ultimate result of stress which creates a general feeling of exhaustion resulting when an individual feels too much pressure, no satisfaction, and decreased escape mechanisms.

21

Stressors may result from three general categories:
1. Organizational;
2. Environmental; and
3. Personal.

24

Wage and salary administration may include these elements:
1. Wage and salary levels and structures;
2. Individual wage determination;
3. Method of payment;
4. Indirect compensation;
5. Exempt employees;
6. Management control; and,
7. Compensation (pay) equity.

23

Equal Pay Act is legislation that:
Prohibits discrimination in pay on the basis of sex of an employee under coverage of the Fair Labor Standards Act.

25

SITUATIONAL MOTIVATION

26

PERFORMANCE APPRAISAL METHODS

+ +

27

OPERANT CONDITIONING

28

THE AMERICANS WITH DISABILITIES
ACT (1990)

+ +

29

PURPOSES OF PERFORMANCE
APPRAISAL

30

STEPS IN PROGRESSIVE DISCIPLINE

26

Methods for employee performance appraisal
include the use of:
- Essay appraisal
- Graphic rating scales
- Checklists
- Forced-choice rating
- Critical incident
- Ranking
- MBO

25

Principles which some theorists believe are needed to
permeate the situation for employees to be motivated are:
- Work must be viewed as personally meaningful.
- People are assigned the responsibility and the account-
  ability for the outcome of their work.
- Individuals are provided with the actual results
  of their efforts (feedback).

28

The Americans with Disabilities Act is legislation
that:
Generates the right of employment to any
job applicant who can perform "essential" job
requirements and requires that firms make
"reasonable accommodations" to help disabled
persons to be able to act, as long as the alternatives can be made without "undue hardship."
(An extension of the Vocational Rehabilitation
Act)

27

Operant conditioning:
1. Known as the Law of Effect
2. Holds the premise that behavior results
   from its consequences
3. Founded by B. F. Skinner

30

The steps in a progressive discipline process
are:
1. Informal discussion;
2. Informal warning;
3. Formal warning;
4. Suspension; and
5. Dismissal.

29

The primary purposes for conducting performance appraisals
on a regular basis relate to:
1. Position decisions;
2. Employee improvements;
3. Coaching; and
4. Counseling.

Study Tip Exam Prep (S.T.E.P.) Card
PART III: ORGANIZATIONS AND MANAGEMENT

Mentally review these terms until you can define them quickly.

1. Bureaucratic theory
2. Decision tree
3. Direct costs
4. Mission statement
5. Chain of command
6. Job casting
7. Indirect costs
8. Organizing
9. Brainwriting
10. Gantt chart
11. Supervision
12. Carrier
13. Advertising media
14. Graphic & charting methods
15. Planning
16. MIS
17. Contingency plan
18. Frequency distribution
19. Responsibility
20. Delphi Technique
21. Administrative management
22. Delegation
23. Advertising
24. Private carrier
25. Therblig
26. Law of the situation
27. Certainty
28. Procedure
29. Exception principle
30. Aggregate planning
31. Piggyback service
32. Quality control
33. Common carrier
34. Marketing mix
35. Hawthorne studies
36. Cost-oriented pricing
37. Classical management theory
38. Distribution
39. Unity of direction
40. Esprit de corp
41. Acceptance theory
42. Hierachy of needs
43. Performance standards
44. Process costing
45. Theory X
46. Production era
47. Operations research
48. Concurrent controls
49. Principle
50. Behavioral science research
51. Scalar principle
52. Committee
53. Rule
54. Span of control
55. Authority
56. Lead time
57. Fishyback service
58. Promotional mix
59. Marketing channel
60. Scientific management
61. Primary data source
62. Direct transfer of title
63. Industrial users
64. Personal selling
65. Transportation time
66. Private carrier
67. Electronic mail
68. Four P's of marketing
69. Feedback controls
70. Pipeline transportation
71. Clayton act
72. Ultimate consumers
73. Theory Y
74. TQM
75. Closed system
76. Human relations theory
77. Budget
78. PERT
79. Standard
80. Sponsor
81. Market
82. Marketing
83. Centralization
84. Theory Z
85. Inputs
86. Management science theory
87. Inspection
88. Intuition
89. Job
90. Secondary data source
91. HR management theory
92. Contact carrier
93. Policy
94. Controlling
95. Brainstorming
96. Customer-oriented pricing
97. Competition-oriented pricing
98. CSM
99. Consolidated delivery system
100. Decision criteria

Study Tip Exam Prep (S.T.E.P.) Card
PART III: ORGANIZATIONS AND MANAGEMENT

Mentally review these terms until you can define them quickly.

1. Bureaucratic theory
2. Decision tree
3. Direct costs
4. Mission statement
5. Chain of command
6. Job costing
7. Indirect costs
8. Organizing
9. Brainwriting
10. Gantt chart
11. Supervisor
12. Carrier
13. Advertising media
14. Graphic & charting methods
15. Planning
16. MIS
17. Contingency plan
18. Frequency distribution
19. Responsibility
20. Delphi Technique
21. Administrative management
22. Delegation
23. Advertising
24. Private carrier
25. Therblig
26. Law of the situation
27. Certainty
28. Procedure
29. Exception principle
30. Aggregate planning
31. Piggyback service
32. Quality control
33. Common carrier
34. Marketing mix
35. Hawthorne studies
36. Cost-oriented pricing
37. Classical management theory
38. Distribution
39. Unity of direction
40. Esprit de corp
41. Acceptance theory
42. Hierarchy of needs
43. Performance standards
44. Process costing
45. Theory X
46. Production era
47. Operations research
48. Concurrent controls
49. Principle
50. Behavioral science research
51. Scalar principle
52. Committee
53. Rule
54. Span of control
55. Authority
56. Lead time
57. Fishyback service
58. Promotional mix
59. Marketing channel
60. Scientific management
61. Primary data source
62. Direct transfer of title
63. Industrial users
64. Personal selling
65. Transportation time
66. Private carrier
67. Electronic mail
68. Four P's of marketing
69. Feedback controls
70. Pipeline transportation
71. Clayton Act
72. Ultimate consumers
73. Theory Y
74. TQM
75. Closed system
76. Human relations theory
77. Budget
78. PERT
79. Standard
80. Sponsor
81. Market
82. Marketing
83. Centralization
84. Theory Z
85. Inputs
86. Management science theory
87. Inspection
88. Intuition
89. Job
90. Secondary data source
91. HR management theory
92. Contract carrier
93. Policy
94. Controlling
95. Brainstorming
96. Customer-oriented pricing
97. Competition-oriented pricing
98. CSM
99. Consolidated delivery system
100. Decision criteria

1

FREDERICK W. TAYLOR

2

TYPES OF CONFLICT

3

TYPES OF FEEDBACK

4

LILLIAN AND FRANK GILBRETH

5

FREQUENCY DISTRIBUTION

6

MANAGEMENT THEORIES

2

The three types of conflict are:

1. Topic;

2. Interpersonal; and

3. Combination (multilevel).

1

THE FATHER OF SCIENTIFIC MANAGEMENT

+ +

4

Known for work in:

1. Motion study;

2. Work methods; and

3. Coined word "Therblig."

3

Two basic types of feedback are:

1. Direct; and

2. Delayed.

+ +

6

Three management theories are:

1. Scientific management;

2. Administrative management; and

3. Bureaucratic theory.

5

Frequency distribution;

1. Chart of information in table format;

2. Illustrates number of times an item appears in comparison to other items; and

3. Provides a system for statisticians to use to develop inferences and predictions.

7

8

EFFECTIVE ELEMENTS OF INVENTORY
REPLENISHMENT POLICIES

HENRY L. GANTT

+ +

9

10

ECONOMIC ORDER QUANTITY

WILLIAM H. LEFFINGWELL

+ +

11

12

BASIC TYPES OF INVENTORIES

HENRI FAYOL

8

The Gantt chart is a graphic aid to allow management to plan and control operations more efficiently.

7

The elements of effective inventory replenishment policies include:
1. Costs;
2. Inventory planning;
3. Quantity discounts; and
4. Timing.

+ +

10

William N. Leffingwell is known as the:
1. Father of office management; and,
2. Authored *Scientific Office Management.*

9

The EOQ formula identifies:
1. How much should be ordered; and
2. When to order to meet estimated demand at the lowest cost.

+ +

12

Henri Fayol is known as the:
1. Father of administrative management; and
2. Founder of general theory of management which included three types of information:
   • generic activities
   • management elements
   • general principles of management

11

The two basic types of inventories are:
1. Manufacturing; and
2. Distribution.

13

ELEMENTS OF QUALITY CONTROL

14

HAWTHORNE STUDIES
(ELTON MAYO)

15

THE LAW OF THE SITUATION
(MARY PARKER FOLLETT)

16

MARKETING MANAGEMENT

17

TYPES OF CARRIERS

18

RENSIS LIKERT

14

Hawthorne studies:
1. Conducted at Western Electric Company
   (Cicero, IL)
2. Results represented turning point in
   management thought
3. Major conclusions:
   • Recognition at the human element
   • Importance of social relationships

13

The elements of quality control involve:
1. Measurement;
2. Feedback;
3. Comparison with established standards; and
4. Correction when necessary.

16

Marketing management means making decisions
about:
1. Products;
2. Distribution;
3. Promotion;
4. Prices; and
5. Sales.

15

Concepts of this research on leadership proposed:
1. Internal factors present with the leader himself/herself;
2. Those factors present within the subordinate; and
3. Those factors present within and related to the situation
   have significant impact upon what constitutes effective
   leadership.

18

Four leadership system includes these styles:
1. Exploitative authoritative style;
2. Benevolent authoritative style;
3. Consultative style; and
4. Participative style.

17

The three types of carriers are:
1. Common
2. Contract; and
3. Private.

19

PHYSICAL DISTRIBUTION

20

PHILIP CROSBY'S FOUR ABSOLUTES
OF QUALITY

21

THREE METHODS FOR DATA
COLLECTION

22

THREE BASIC PREMISES OF TQM

23

MARKET ANALYSIS

24

STRATEGIC PLANS

20

Philip Crosby's four absolutes of quality are:
1. A definition;
2. A system;
3. A standard for performance; and
4. A method for measuring quality.

19

Physical distribution is the total process of:
1. moving;
2. handling; and
3. storing
goods on the way from the producers to the users.

22

The three basic premises of TQM are:
1. The satisfaction of multiple customers with products and services;
2. The implementation of employment empowerment; and
3. The use of statistical tools for problem-solving.

21

The three main methods for collecting data are:
1. Survey;
2. Experimental; and
3. Observational.

24

Strategic plans are:
1. Broad and long-term;
2. Guides for the operations of an organization; and
3. Province of upper level management.

23

Market research is involved primarily with finding facts in three areas:
1. Consumer;
2. Competition; and
3. Internal operations.

25

PRODUCT ADVERTISING

26

TACTICAL PLANS

27

THE "FOUR P's" OF MARKETING

28

MANAGEMENT BY OBJECTIVES (MBO)

29

NETWORK PLANNING METHODS

30

RESISTANCE BEHAVIOR

26

Tactical plans are:

1. Intermediate in nature;
2. Aids to achieving the broad objective in strategic plans; and
3. The responsibility of middle level managers.

25

Product advertising can be used to:

1. Support personal selling;
2. Create customer interest in a product or service;
3. Keep the consumer aware of the product/service over a period of time;
4. Introduce a new product or service; and
5. Introduce a new business to the community.

28

Management by Objectives (MBO)

1. Systematic approach to planning and controlling activities;
2. Involves a supervisor-worker collaboration in setting objectives; and
3. Establishes specific goals with measurable outcomes.

27

The "four P's" of marketing are:

1. Product;
2. Price;
3. Place; and
4. Promotion.

30

Resistance behavior (change) may result for the following reasons:

1. Loss of power and prestige;
2. Fear of job elimination;
3. Role ambiguity;
4. Changed relationships; and
5. Changed work patterns.

29

Two popular network planning methods are:

1. Critical Path Method (CPM); and,
2. Performance Evaluation and Review Techniques (PERT).